LONDON'S RIVER

LONDON'S RIVER

WRITTEN AND ILLUSTRATED BY
GEOFFREY S. FLETCHER

HUTCHINSON OF LONDON

HUTCHINSON & CO (*Publishers*) LTD

178–202 Great Portland Street, London W1

London Melbourne Sydney
Auckland Bombay Toronto
Johannesburg New York

★

First published 1966

*This book has been set in Times, printed in Great Britain
on cartridge paper at Taylor Garnett Evans & Co. Ltd,
Watford, Herts by offset litho and bound by Wm. Brendon,
Tiptree, Essex*

Contents

———— * ————

TO ALISON

I

Turner's Greenwich

———— * ————

THIS BOOK is in no sense a history. There are plenty of those already in existence, dealing with the Thames from early pre-Roman times to its present position of forming the largest port on earth, with the greatest area of docks, and showing how the river brought London into existence and then nurtured its fortunes.

Statistical information is also almost entirely lacking in these pages. New and curious information, the product of over twenty years' wandering by the river, sailing up and down on it and living on its shores, there undoubtedly is; but in the main my purpose is to convey as graphically as I can its many scenic qualities. So the Thames is only considered – as I view everything else – as a thing possessing artistic possibilities of form and colour and subtle ideas. I have only a subsidiary interest in the river as a highway (which is what it used formerly to be, far more than

9

today) or in how many million tons of food are carried up and down it annually and Gradgrind facts of that nature.

In fact, the Thames was invented entirely by artists and poets. Oscar Wilde in one of his essays refers to the way Nature copies effects originally invented by artists, and cites Turner and Whistler as examples. It is quite true: Nature and life imitate art quite slavishly. You invent and draw two worn-out characters for a half-penny paper. You call them Weary Willie and Tired Tim. They catch on and henceforth every tramp models himself on them, down to the minutest detail – Nature imitating art.

No sooner had art produced a Davy Crockett, a Jean Harlow, a beatnik, than Nature moved in, bettered the lesson and produced a million from the prototype. When Turner had invented burning sunsets over the river, the Thames went on to repeat them. As Wilde said, London may have had fogs before Whistler, but few noticed them. When Whistler produced his dreamy Nocturnes and lavender river twilights, Nature became charmed with the notion and the Thames has gone on producing them ever since.

To treat all the Thames at all adequately throughout the whole of its length, from its springs in the Cotswolds to its mouth at the Nore would, I imagine, require something like the old-fashioned three-volume publication. For all practical purposes, those reaches of the river beyond Gravesend, where the pilots are dropped, offer little of interest, except in such places as Canvey Island, Leigh and Southend, and one or two on the Kentish shore. The problem was where to end in a westerly direction, leaving the metropolitan – or more accurately the central – Thames for attention. Teddington where it ceases to be tidal seemed to be a suitable boundary, but I felt a little more elbow-room was needed. If I extended my survey to go as far as Windsor, the distance (taking all the windings into consideration) begins to get somewhat too much for detailed handling. Bearing in mind my own predilection for the industrial parts of the river and wishing to make the book generally useful to readers whose opportunities would be mostly confined to central London, I finally decided to take an arbitrary selection from Kingston, where the river becomes definitely rural (and remains so with the exception, mainly, of Reading), down to Woolwich, after which its interest from my point of view is more sporadic.

In between these points, I have drawn and discussed a selection of those things that interest me and which I hope will interest readers too. The dual character of the Thames is very striking. The Seine, on the other hand, contrives to keep up a rural character alongside its industrial commitments, so to speak. If you compare its graceful sweep round the Isle de la Cité, where the water sparkles below shady trees and creeper covered embankments, with its counterpart on the Thames below St Paul's, you will acknowledge that the Thames is more departmentalized in the conduct of its affairs. Not that the rural Thames comes to a full stop – a sudden pull up – all at once. For instance, it is industrialized at Hammersmith, but

10

becomes countrified for a while at Barn Elms. Putney is mixed, neither one thing nor the other, but certainly not grim, after which the river becomes oppressive at Wandsworth, only to take on a period charm as it flows between Battersea Bridge and Chelsea Bridge, where the river throws off all traces of its country origin and becomes at last, at Lambeth, a downright Cockney.

In my *London Nobody Knows*, I made the comment that, though London had been well served by artists and writers, it had never been intimately, indissolubly associated with the work of a significant artist of the quality of Meryon and Baudelaire. I might have gone further to make the point that much of the pictorial art connected with London is topographical. I can think of notable exceptions to this, as in the work of Sickert and the group round him. Nevertheless, in general, most London art has been objective, topographical art having the making of a record as its primary aim. A tremendous volume of work has resulted to delight the eye by fine draughtsmanship and to supply us, the inheritors of a much meaner city, with reliable information about its architecture and life at earlier periods. In passing, it is interesting to speculate on the kind of subject Meryon would have chosen for a series of architectural plates on the Thames similar to his monumental set etched in Paris in the early 1850s. These, confined mainly to the neighbourhood of the Cité, include several river subjects – the Petit Pont, the Morgue (vividly described by Dickens), the Pont au Change, the Pont Neuf and the superb etching of the apse of Notre Dame. In these the peculiar light of Paris is caught along with the mystery and grandeur of ancient buildings and a subtle undertone of disquiet which permeates the whole, river as well as architecture.

To judge from the evidence of the plates, Meryon would certainly have etched London Bridge, for its Piranesi-like austerity echoes that of the Pont Neuf and other bridges in this area round the Cité, and he might well have paralleled the Morgue by an etching of the Millbank Penitentiary, on the site now occupied by the Tate Gallery. Though evidently strongly drawn towards Gothic architecture, he would, I fancy, have left the Palace of Westminster alone; admirable as it is, it had not then the impress of years on it. In fact it was still under construction in the early 'fifties, and I believe he would have preferred the Abbey from a point on the Lambeth side, as Peter de Wint saw it, when worn-out, picturesque old houses still fringed the river at the foot of Lambeth Bridge. Obviously Meryon would have seen the possibilities of the Lion Brewery. The façade of great columns with the lion above and the mud below was not unlike his etching of the Ministry of Marine, apart from the flying fish in the sky which no one ever witnessed over the Brewery.

The demolition of the Lion Brewery was an outstanding architectural loss to the Thames. It ought to have been preserved and restored and made the water entrance to the concert hall – not, of course, the Festival Hall as it now stands, already dated and of clumsy outline and proportion, but one designed to harmonize with the restored, rehabilitated Brewery. As things are now, the whole area is one of inconceivable mediocrity and unsurpassed dullness, tinged with the insufferable socialist, better-Britain flavour of the period. Fortunately, the Lion Brewery was the subject of an etching by James McBey, in which not a little of Meryon's feeling for the enigmatic qualities of architecture appears. Here, incidentally, it may be worth adding that a variety of relics were found on the site of the Brewery, which adjoined the Coade artificial stone works where the Lion was cast. I went over the site with the engineer in charge and saw the collection of old tobacco pipes and oak drain pipes turned up in the excavations. The lion, rescued at the request of King George VI, is now mounted on a pedestal by Westminster Bridge. He had his belly examined during his removal; it was found to be empty, apart from a bottle. (That the British Lion is hollow-bellied was suspected by foreigners for years before he took to National Health teeth.) The hope that the bottle contained the long-forgotten formula for the manufacture of Coade stone proved groundless; there was only some dull, pointless message, as with most bottles. The lion has a relative, originally on the Brewery entrance and now stored in the basement of County Hall.

Before this digression, I remarked that London-inspired art was in the main topographical. To enumerate those artists who have (as second-rate writers used to say) received inspiration from the Thames would fill this book, but a short list will indicate the extent. Foreigners I exclude, though one must not forget the Thames subjects painted by the Impressionists during their period in London during the Franco-Prussian War. Sisley painted the regatta on the Thames (now in the Louvre) and Claude Monet the Houses of Parliament and other views of Westminster during this period in London and also at the beginning of the present century.

Hollar comes first, with his etched views of the river as it appeared in the seventeenth century. Rembrandt probably based his drawing of Old St Paul's from the south side of the river on a Hollar etching – or one of Hollar's many followers from the Low Countries who produced a quantity of panoramic views of the Thames at this period, for there is no reliable evidence that Rembrandt ever visited London.

But another foreigner did – Canaletto – and to his employment in London we owe much of our knowledge of London as it appeared after Wren had left it, a city of sunlit spires with a skyline of rare beauty, fit to suggest a New Jerusalem. These drawings at Windsor and the paintings associated with them show this City skyline as Wren intended it to be seen; a debased version of this prospect could be seen until comparatively recent years from Waterloo Bridge, but the hideous office blocks which began to appear in the late 1950s completed the work of degradation. Londoners ought to get wild with anger at this insolence, but they never do nowadays. Those who manipulate them have taken care to hedge them in with penal laws and twisted explanations: few Londoners, as a result, know or care about anything, a point I shall have reason to revert to when discussing

London Bridge. Canaletto worked in London in the mid-eighteenth century, and the drawings include various views of Westminster, showing the then new church of St John the Evangelist, Smith Square by Archer (the 'very hideous church' known as 'Queen Anne's Footstool' in the centre of the square where Jenny Wren, the dolls' dressmaker, lived), Westminster Hall, St Margaret's and Old Westminster Bridge, then being under construction. His view of the City from the terrace of Somerset House shows a stretch of placid river and the towers of the City marching, as it were, with St Paul's Cathedral at their head. Canaletto places us as spectators just above the balustrade of the terrace in the sunshine, where some ladies and gentlemen and a chubby curly-tailed dog enjoy the charming prospect. Richly decorated barges make their dignified way in these drawings, small sailing boats catch the sunlight on their canvas, ladies and their escorts have time for leisurely enjoyment of the scenes, the beauties of which are pointed out by the gallants with their walking-sticks.

The Thames was, in fact, the centre of London life, and Canaletto in a considerable number of paintings and drawings reproduced it with its freshness and elegance intact to a degree beyond the powers of his English contemporaries, though of those who followed the fashion set by the Venetian a few such as Marlow and Samuel Scott came at times very close to Canaletto's virtuosity in paint and his luminous treatment of the play of light.

From the end of the eighteenth century, when the great period was beginning, one can choose Rowlandson, who in a number of brilliant drawings portrayed the life of the river from the elegancies of Vauxhall and Ranelagh to the Deptford Dockyard. One of the liveliest, the 'Landing at Greenwich', shows a collection of picturesque houses on either side of the stairs, on the spot where Greenwich Pier now stands; the Hospital is in the distance; up the stairs swarms a boat's crew, with more arriving in a long boat just grounded! Jack 'is home from the sea, and his faithful Nancy, in her haste to offer him her buxom charms, has already tumbled into the boat; Jacks and Nancys swarm everywhere, kissing and cuddling, showing an assortment of well-upholstered arms, legs and breasts like monster balloons. As Dickens said, they were always waiting for him, Mercantile Jack or Jack Tar, ready to help him empty his pockets and give him a dose of pox. They still are.

Constable chose a Thames subject for one of his most ambitious works, 'The Opening of Waterloo Bridge', to which he doubtless was attracted by patriotic feeling, a pride in national achievement which even artists sometimes feel. However, the painting, after many alterations, failed to satisfy the artist, possibly because the original idea was more emotional than pictorial. The first pencil study in the Victoria and Albert Museum shows a wide stretch of river and Waterloo Bridge in the distance, on a high horizon. Ultimately a lower horizon was chosen and part of the garden and terrace of Pembroke House, Whitehall Stairs, included, and a group of state barges – compositional devices which in reality serve only to encumber the design – added in the foreground. The Shot Tower, a Thames land-mark that ought to have been preserved, appears in the distance on the right.

Another, and more conventionally successful, painting of a ceremonial opening was by Clarkson Stanfield, a professional marine painter who recorded the opening of the new London Bridge from a point on Bankside.

But the poetry, the interpretation of the ever-changing moods of the river, came with Turner. One of his earliest exhibited oil paintings, dating from 1797, is of moonlight at Millbank, somewhat after the Dutch manner. Between that and the unforgettable 'Fighting *Téméraire*' – his last important Thames subject with the exception of 'Rain, steam and speed' (the viaduct crossing the Thames at Maidenhead) – came a series of drawings, watercolours, engravings and oil paintings interpreting the genius loci of the river with a profound understanding of its character and a feeling for mood and atmosphere entirely new. The subjects range from Oxford – 'The Union of the Thames and Isis' – to the mouth of the Thames, each reflecting the varied aspects of the river and with subtle rendering of the different depths and movements of its waters. Since its first exhibition in 1839, 'The Fighting *Téméraire*' has been generally accepted as Turner's finest river subject. Its unusual appeal is on the same grounds as the plays of Shake-speare; there is something in it for everyone, the ignorant and intelligent alike, whether they are familiar with the Thames or not.

Thackeray wrote, 'The old *Téméraire* is dragged to her last home by a little spiteful, diabolical steamer. A mighty red sun, amidst a host of flaming clouds, sinks to rest on one side of the picture, and illumines a river that seems intermin-able . . .' He goes on to praise the wonderful distance such as was never painted before; it is a distance as impossible to analyse as the quality of painting in the water, where Turner has expressed not only the tranquil calm I have myself often witnessed, but also the volume and weight of it, rippling under the burning sky and reflecting a fiery path to the setting sun. No one ever painted the Thames in this way before, nor ever shall again. The river side of Millwall is blue with the mist of the evening closing in, and the contrast between the black and smoking paddle tug and the ghostly battleship symbolizes the passing of the eighteenth century before the onset of the technological age.

'Of all pictures of subjects not visibly involving human pain,' Ruskin says of it, 'this is, I believe, the most pathetic that was ever painted. The utmost pensive-ness which can ordinarily be given to a landscape depends on adjuncts of ruin: but no ruin was ever so affecting as this gliding of the vessel to her grave. . . . Never more shall sunset lay golden robe on her, nor starlight tremble on the waves that part at her gliding.'

He gives some interesting details of the vessel's career worth including here. 'She was the second ship in Nelson's line, and, having little provisions or water on board, was what sailors call "flying light" so as to be able to keep pace with the fast-sailing *Victory*. When the latter drew upon herself all the enemy's fire, the

14

Téméraire tried to pass her, to take it in her stead; but Nelson himself hailed her to keep astern. The *Téméraire* cut away her studding-sails, and held back, receiving the enemy's fire into her bows without returning a shot. Two hours later, she lay with a French seventy-four-gun ship on each side of her, both her prizes, one lashed to her mainmast, and one to her anchor.'

This sense of duty done among ships and those who go down to the sea in them occurs often in Turner's pictures; there is a superb design, among his illustrations to the poems of Samuel Rogers, of Greenwich Hospital seen from the Isle of Dogs (reputedly Wren's favourite view of his great building); the twin domes are viewed almost head on, in parallel perspective; between them in the distance rise the slopes of Greenwich Park. A couple of Thames sailing barges in full sail (1,000 square feet of canvas, one of the largest spreads handled by two men) move in on the right. On top of the steps in the foreground is a Greenwich pensioner with his three-cornered hat and a bottle of grog. Behind him is a telescope on a tripod: no doubt he will presently let the ladies who are arriving by boat peer through it for a trifle. Rogers's poetry is indifferent stuff, and has survived only by association with Turner's designs, but the lines illustrated have a period flavour which makes them worth quoting in connexion with the river.

> Go, with old Thames, view Chelsea's glorious pile;
> And ask the shattered hero, whence his smile?
> Go, view the splendid domes of Greenwich – Go,
> And own what raptures from Reflection flow
> Hail, noblest structures imaged in the wave!
> A nation's grateful tribute to the brave.
> Hail, blest retreats from war and shipwreck, hail!
> That oft arrest the wondering stranger's sail.

But the grateful nation saw occasion to move the old sailors out, later on in the century, in spite of the opposition of Ruskin and others, and Greenwich has never been the same since. To bring the pensioners back would do much to assist that revival of Greenwich life which began a few years ago with the berthing of the *Cutty Sark*; Greenwich for years after the war had a depressing air of gloom and lassitude about it. Now that the Trafalgar Tavern has been restored to life, the restoration of the pensioners would be a fit and proper accompaniment. Chelsea fared better in retaining its old soldiers. They add character to its streets, as their uniform adds colour, and there are few sights more agreeable than a Chelsea pub interior when one or two of the old boys sit quietly over their pints of bitter, among the bearded and long-haired youngsters of both sexes and those who occupy the sexual no-man's (or no-woman's)-land. I used often to study them in this way when I lived in Chelsea, always wondering what these antique heroes were thinking: are they critical of the deadbeats; do they moan the changed times and manners and wonder, like the boy on the field of Blenheim, what became of it in the end?

15

A visit to their quarters in Chelsea Hospital, too, is interesting – not only for the superb domestic architecture of Wren, but also as a rare experiment with time. There is no one so neat, so orderly, as your old soldier or sailor, and at Chelsea the pensioners' quarters are models of neatness and compression. You can turn a blind eye to the wireless sets some of them unaccountably have, and the sight of the old fellows in their chapel or dining-room or sitting swapping yarns on the benches along the covered ways is a balm strongly recommended against the chafing effect of contemporary London. It is as if Herkomer's famous Victorian picture had suddenly come to life.

Each time I have visited the hospital, however, I have come away with misgivings. I wonder how long it will be before some rationalizing meddler decides (for the general good, of course) that the old chaps are insulted by wearing a period uniform, that they are made to look buffoons by bright coats, brass buttons and three-cornered or shako-shaped hats, and so agitates until the pensioners are brought into line, compelled to wear denims and have berets clapped on their ancient heads. As I have confessed elsewhere, the same worry troubles me over the Salvation Army, and I had apprehensions over the Boys' Brigade (fears that the black-and-white pillbox of the 1880s would be given up) and I was right. Certainly, the Chelsea Hospital traditions are well rooted in the past and have proved their efficiency long ago, but that is no guarantee of continuity nowadays: all such institutions, particularly where uniqueness is concerned, are at the mercy of the reformers and progressives, and marked by somebody for cutting down in the war between mediocrities and those who still prize originality. The Governor's quarters are in that blend of solid restrained grandeur and comfort so well handled by Wren. As might be expected, there are a number of loyal portraits.

To revert to Greenwich and Turner. Turner made several views of the Hospital. One, based on pencil drawings, is in the Liber Studiorum, and the artist also carried out the same subject in a painting. A few years ago I was curious enough to try to identify the spot in Greenwich Park overlooking the Hospital and river from which the drawing was made, and to my pleasure I found that, in spite of the passage of a century and a quarter, the spot could be narrowed down to within a few yards. The various architectural features – St Paul's dome, the domes of the Hospital and Greenwich Church – formed fixed points of calculation. Turner did very little in the way of artistic reshaping, mainly clearing up the confusion of roofs and parapets round the Hospital and emphasizing very slightly the slow, graceful curve of the river as it sweeps round the Isle of Dogs.

In the first decade of the nineteenth century, Turner spent a lot of time on the lower reaches of the Thames, filling a number of sketchbooks with shipping studies – ships of the line, Thames barges and wherries at places such as Purfleet, Greenwich and Southend. Besides these, there was the superb series of oil studies on panel, direct from Nature and anticipating Constable, painted on the rural reaches – 'The Thames near Walton Bridges' in the National Gallery is an example;

reenwich foreshore

and there were those limpid, halcyon subjects from the Liber Studiorum such as the so-called 'Pope's Villa' and the drawing of the boys angling, the latter no doubt seen by the artist in the neighbourhood of his house (now demolished) in Hammersmith Mall.

A visit to Greenwich Hospital, a study of its colonnades and other architectural features and the majestic grouping of the whole is in itself a liberal education. This part of the river is dominated by the sheer splendour of the façade, even from a distance away as in my drawing of the foreshore with the great iron piers of the power station on the previous page. From the river, or even from the riverside promenade, the grandeur of Wren's planning can be immediately appreciated; it is worthy of Venice and Rome and shows his absolute mastery over form and space. The building is pure Baroque, and Wren, with great skill, contrived to use it as a frame for Inigo Jones's Queen's House in the distance below the slope of Greenwich Park, which forms the exquisite focal point of the whole. Wren's two assistants, Vanbrugh and Hawksmoor, also worked at Greenwich; they, with Thomas Archer (another of Wren's assistants), Gibbs and Thornhill constitute the chief exponents of the Baroque in England. Sir James Thornhill, the father-in-law of Hogarth, painted the remarkable murals at Greenwich (his other main work in London being the grisaille paintings in the dome of St Paul's). He was a true master of the Baroque and an isolated one, for English patrons usually commissioned foreigners.

In a word, Greenwich Hospital is one of the most notable examples of the Baroque, and has a refinement about it often missing in Continental Baroque, where theatricality and architectural posturing often crept in in the prevailing atmosphere of the Counter-Reformation. Besides, there is a charming contrast between all this restrained magnificence and the humbler buildings of the riverfront – cottages and pubs – only the English contrive such combinations so successfully.

One of London's sharpest contrasts is that between the Trinity almshouses of early Gothic Revival design, like a boy's fort, with ivy-covered garden walls and clipped hollies, and the overwhelming bulk of the Power Station immediately next to it. Unfeeling as architects and engineers often are, it is difficult to imagine any so indifferent as to deposit this basely ugly heap next to so fragile a toy, not to mention the entire absence of harmony between it and Greenwich Hospital.

There is a high tide mark on the river wall opposite the almshouses and seats on the grass where old men doze or watch the ships passing up and down Greenwich Reach. Then the open space closes in again to the alley behind the Trafalgar Tavern, Crane Street, where the blue and white paint and bright curtains of the cottages give a pleasant sea-going sort of flavour – a messing about in boats: the twin domes of the Hospital rise above the chimney pots and TV aerials. However, before turning down the alley, there are other waterfront pleasures to be experienced. These consist of the handsome, late Georgian pub, the Cutty Sark, and the row of houses (pure old London and quite delightful) next to it. Approach it from under the Power Station wharf and the alley twisting between the scrap-yards. Before 1954, the pub was named the Union. It is a free house and dates from about 1805, occupying the site of an ancient beer house known as the Green Man. The bar is old-fashioned, wooden-panelled and inviting, and if you want to enjoy a whitebait supper (a Greenwich tradition), the bow-windowed dining-room upstairs provides this in a plain, honest style, and draught Guinness, too, if you wish. Only, the whitebait are no longer taken out of the river at Greenwich as they were in Dickens' time: oil from the ship's bilges and the muck that clandestinely goes into the river has changed all that, though the river was clear as recently as forty years ago. Sixty years and more ago the bargemen used Thames water for drinking purposes (as I have been told by ancients along the river), lowering a can from the barges and various water plants flourished at the edge of the tide. Now there are no whitebait nearer than Southend and no vegetation apart from cabbage stalks.

Between courses, you can sit on the ample seats under the window and look out over the river to the Waterman's Arms and the church spire on the Isle of Dogs. You can watch the evening mist falling over the river, modulating stronger colours in to a variety of subtle greys – darks inside the hulls of barges, flat greys of distant warehouses and wide spaces of pinky grey sky reflected in the slowly rippling water. There are touches of dull reds on the barges and notes of green among the tarpaulins. Lights string out along the shore or on the ships or wink on groups of barges. When you are familiar with the lights of the river, you can be sure of your position from them, even on dead, black nights when the moon is hiding her face. The little group of houses belong to Morden College, and they rarely change hands; two have pretty wooden balconies. Beyond, the Harbour Master's house closes up the view among the ships' masts, smoking chimneys and gasometers.

If your mood is for something grand, the Trafalgar is your tavern. Its recent restoration, after years of neglect, cost a fortune, and, besides being a business proposition, was an act of piety for the Trafalgar is one of the great historic taverns of the nineteenth century and architecturally one of the most important in London. My drawing was made just before the restoration began, as I thought it interesting to record it in its unredeemed condition. Dickens would have rejoiced at its remarkable transformation. He was a frequent visitor: his last meeting with Douglas Jerrold took place here, and Bella Wilfer, who had just become Mrs John Rokesmith in Greenwich Church, chose it for her wedding breakfast: '. . . that dinner in the very room of the very hotel' where she and her father had once dined together when 'everything was delightful. The Park was delightful, the punch was delightful, the dishes of fish were delightful, the wine was delight-ful'. And the little room overlooking the river into which they were shown for dinner was delightful!

The Trafalgar Tavern was designed by John Kay, surveyor to Greenwich Hospital, and built in 1837. It had many rooms and banqueting halls, each named after a naval hero, and became famous for its ministerial whitebait dinners – the opposition going to the now vanished Ship. The Liberals under Mr Gladstone held their last dinner there in 1883, and it was the custom for the Government to go down river to Greenwich in a steamer-bedecked ordnance barge, though more prosaic steamers had taken over from the barges by the time the custom was dropped. During the whitebait season, the hotel stables were crowded with horses, and four-in-hand coaches, drags and carriages would line Park Row as far as the park gate. Today the road is lined with the cars of well-groomed clients who enjoy once more the pleasures of a riverside dinner. A doorman in uniform directs affairs outside, though, for my part, I would have him dressed like Nelson: I might even insist on employing a one-eyed, one-armed man for the part. That at least is what a thorough-going public relations man would dream up, and I have a warm affection for their contrivances, their concocted events. The Trafalgar closed in 1908, and was then used for several purposes until being converted into flats in 1936. Part of the east wing houses the Curlew Rowing Club, one of the old river clubs 'below bridges'. The best time to see the restored Trafalgar is at dusk, when there is still enough light to appreciate the colour scheme of pale duck-egg blue, white and black and the graceful, elliptical curves of the windows overlooking the river, particularly if the tide is full, breaking up the orange lights of the windows in Impressionistic reflections.

In the heyday of Greenwich, there were other riverside taverns – the Ship (a rival claimant to the Trafalgar in connexion with *Our Mutual Friend*) and the Crown and Sceptre. The Ship, destroyed by bombing in November 1941, was also, as I have said, famous for its fish dinners. For the uninitiated, I may add that whitebait are no distinct species of fish; they are immature fish of all kinds, mainly herring and sprats, in sizes varying from a tadpole to a small goldfish, caught fresh and fried with tails, heads and eyes complete. The *Cutty Sark*, in its dry dock, occupies the site of the Ship. My drawing at the beginning of this chapter was made in an autumn sunset immediately before a storm: the clipper was a black silhouette against smouldering clouds, and a red sky shone through the glass dome of the entrance to Greenwich Tunnel.

Dumping a power station on this delightful stretch of the waterfront was one of the worst riverside crimes of London. However, the huge metal columns and the grimy coaling wharf they support over the muddy beach frame an admirable view of the riverside as it curves round the Hospital. The very gauntness of the rusty ironwork – at present (1965) being repainted – focuses attention on the elegant façade of the Trafalgar and on the architecture of the Hospital, and the

21

riverside trees are soft and delicately green in the spring sunshine. The *Cutty Sark* has added immensely to the pictorial effects over a wide area of Greenwich: one sees its masts unexpectedly above house tops and round the corners of narrow passages. It suggests the appearance of the river in the last century, prompting the reflection that artists interested in the river today live in a bleak period. The romance might still be there – though this is open to doubt – but the wonderful opportunities supplied by sailing ships and paddle boats is entirely lacking. Those who drew and painted the Thames in the nineteenth century had most of their work done for them. Tissot, for instance; think of his paintings on board ship – the curves of rail and woodwork which he so obviously delights to use, echoing them by the shapes of cane chairs and the curvation of pretty girls as they look over the handrails; all this admirable material was used to the full by Tissot, as it was by the Impressionists. It is not going too far to say that a good deal of the enjoyment we get from their paintings is due to delightful costume – bustles, straw boaters, striped silks, parasols and so on – quite as much as from purely aesthetic considerations. Association, too, influences our judgement to a considerable extent in these pictures of what now seems a golden age. Under its spell, even mediocre artists produced enviable work – Joseph Pennell, for instance, made delightful drawings of the lower reaches of the Thames. Napier Hemy, a now almost forgotten painter, was at his best in Limehouse. Basil Bradley, now entirely forgotten, painted charmingly on the upper reaches of the river, where willows shaded banks of cow parsley and youths with walrus moustaches, caps and striped blazers escorted the maidens that du Maurier drew – idylls recalling James Thompson's 'Sunday up the River':

> My love o'er the water bends dreaming;
> It glideth and glideth away:
> She sees there her own beauty, gleaming
> Through shadow and ripple and spray
>
> O tell her, thou murmuring river,
> As past her your light wavelets roll,
> How steadfast that image for ever
> Shines pure in pure depths of my soul.

Mortimer Menpes, too, follower and pupil of Whistler and a chronically feeble artist, was buoyed up, as it were, by the river, and thereby produced some respectable work. (He even opened a creamery and dairy at Pangbourne: I went in search of it once, when studying Edwardian dairies, but I found it had become a bicycle shop.)

Greenwich Church was designed by John James and dates from the beginning of the eighteenth century. It is dedicated to St Alphege who was martyred here by the Danes. The church sustained much damage during the war, but was skilfully restored by my old friend and tutor, Sir A. E. Richardson. The exterior

22

remained intact, most of the damage being done to the interior which is almost entirely new. The woodwork is now beginning to tone down. There is some cunning imitative painting on the chancel arch – trophies and a simulated coffered ceiling in brown and gold, very much in the spirit of similar eighteenth-century work. I remember when the plasterwork of the great oval ceiling was being cast (from moulds copied from salvaged fragments) and the high standard of plaster work which Richardson exacted, the work being carried to a degree of finish almost in excess of necessity. This was in contrast to modern plaster work in some restored city churches, which only passed muster when erected in position. Richardson's lamps, sticking up from among the pews, are, however, a mistake. General Gordon was baptized here in 1833 and General Wolfe buried in the church on 20 November 1759.

Once I went into Greenwich Church to find a man in a cloth cap eating an ice cream.

I said, 'You've got your head covered, and you happen to be in church.'

'So what?'

'So it's an impertinence, and what's more you've no business to be eating here, either.'

'Nobody minds.'

'You may think so, but I disapprove *and so does God.*'

As he made no reply and continued to suck the slider, I twisted it out of his paws on to the floor, knocked his cap off his head and threw it down the church. The villain was so taken aback, he seemed paralysed by surprise. It compares with a notice I saw this summer (1965) in the porch of All Hallows by the Tower, addressed to the rubbernecks: 'You are requested to smoke your cigarettes and consume your ices outside the church.'

There's a nice old terrace of Bloomsbury-like character near the church and a little National School worth noting, and on the other side is the Mitre Hotel, a dignified early Victorian building of grey brick with pedimented and square headed windows. Victorian-type lettering on the sign board, fixed against the angles of the wall, gives an extra period flavour.

It is time now to move down to Woolwich, through the sad lands of East Greenwich and into a landscape undergoing a face-lift in the shape of towering blocks of housing developments. But before going, take time off to go up Stockwell Street to Spread Eagle Yard where the coaches once left for Charing Cross. The coach office is now an antique shop, which, however, has much to offer in the way of 'junk'. Here you will find Edwardian picture postcards, magic lantern slides, stereoscope pictures, prints, posters and old toys. In fact, there is no knowing what you will find – a chamber pot which will go bump in the night might be your delightful discovery, a pre-Great War Cadbury's chocolate box with *Gloire de Dijon* roses on the lid, a case of stuffed birds, perhaps, or a tray full of glass eyes which you could buy for your small boy to use as marbles: there is always something new and intriguing.

Opposite is the old Parthenon Music Hall, which began life as Crowder's Music Hall, then became the Parthenon and, after the Great War, emerged as the Hippodrome Cinema. Now, as this book is being written, the place is entering on a new phase – or it will do so when the rebuilding is complete – as the Greenwich Theatre. My drawing of the interior (one of the smallest in London) shows part of the boxes and the proscenium arch, which is to be retained. The pretty galleries were too far gone to be kept, and the fire exits from them too risky for modern licensing authorities. This revival of the theatre is another satisfactory aspect of the Greenwich Renaissance.

While Greenwich has gone up, Woolwich has gone down. Its chief attraction, the delightful paddle boats of the free ferry, on the decks of which I have spent many a blissful afternoon, crossing and recrossing the Thames for nothing, are a thing of the past. But knowing their destiny and knowing I should deplore the new ones, whatever improved service they might offer, I made a drawing (which appears as the frontispiece) before the last of the old boats disappeared which captures their character very completely.

Part of the Parish of Woolwich lies on the northern side of the river, for some inexplicable reason, and the parishioners had the right to run a ferry from a very early period. As Woolwich developed, the existing means of crossing the river by small boats became inadequate, and eventually in 1889 the Woolwich Free Ferry was opened by the Metropolitan Board of Works. The cost was £192,000 and since then the ferry has only been closed once, for about three months in 1949. Sir Joseph Bazalgette, the great Victorian engineer who also planned the Embankment, did his work well. The original paddle boats, one of which was still working in 1930, cost £45,000 each. The four which replaced them and which have themselves been scrapped were all built in the Isle of Wight, and arrived at Woolwich under their own steam. These four (I forget which one I drew, but they were almost identical) were the paddle steamers *Gordon* (built 1923), the *Squires* (1922) and the *John Benn* and *Will Crooks* (both built in 1930). Their propelling machinery was unique. Each boat had two boilers, one at each end. They were coke-fired by hand stoking, and worked at a pressure of 60 lbs per square inch. The engines were two-cylindered steam-condensing engines, suitable for quick manoeuvering. But the pressure of modern traffic, the chronic delays at the ferry, not to mention the wearing out of the boats and the disappearance of all romance from London, spelt their doom. One of the new boats is called *Ernest Bevin*. Another, *John Burns*, is bad enough, but *Ernest Bevin* is surely the ultimate depth of soulless, socialist drabness.

Perhaps Londoners can consider themselves lucky that no new boat has as yet been christened 'Herbert Morrison'. Apart from Bevin, I can think of nothing more dreary. There was at least this to be said for Bevin: embarrassing as he was,

24

he did not play a leading part in tearing down the old Waterloo Bridge or in replacing it by the present, straight-backed monster, nor did he have his ashes tipped into the Thames. Needless to say, the boats, old or new, have all been poorly, unimaginatively named. The 'General Gordon' would have been suitable, the 'Artilleryman', too, perhaps, or even the 'Woolwich Belle', but only a bureaucrat, and a Socialist one at that, could have forced out 'Ernest Bevin' from his exuberant fancy.

What delighted us, of course, about these paddle boats (which, incidentally, consumed 100 tons of coke a week) was their resemblance to those Mississippi steamboats of *Life on the Mississippi* and *Huckleberry Finn*. When the northern bound vessel crossed the path of the one returning to Woolwich, the effect was pure Mark Twain. The new boats are more efficient, but the charm has clean gone from the ferry. What is the use of pretending to be a Mississippi gambler – a Creole lady on each knee, a revolver in one hand, and a glass of mint julep with your poker cards in the other – on board the 'Ernie Bevin'?

Thousands of houses were built in Woolwich during the Great War for munition workers in the Arsenal. Now the Arsenal itself is to be redeveloped – a thousand acres of it – and the result will be virtually a new town. Woolwich has one redeeming feature which still makes the place worth a visit, the street market, at its best on Saturday, in Beresford Square. The pavement goes down in steps behind the stalls, and discarded vegetables, coloured tissue paper and boxes flow down, a sort of waterfall of rubbish, into the road. Here a persuasive patterer offers bedding-out plants and pots of American chrysanthemums. 'Who wants another nice pot o' 'mums for 3/-? This one's a smasher. Two more to go. Give us three shillings for the other one. That's a nice one. Luvly 'mums, lidy . . . Nah then, wot else d'yer want? Marigolds, my dear? Authentic French marigolds – a shillin'.' Hopeful pigeons flutter down among the purple paper and garbage. '. . . Pashun flower, a shillin' . . . shillin' blue, oh, it's a smasher, lidy, look at that wun . . . orl ready for goin' outdoors. Who wants two more genuine French marigolds? None of yer imitashun marigolds 'ere. They're orl genuine and honly a shillin' a pair.'

There are toy stalls, too, button, cotton and silk stalls, grocery stalls with huge cheeses, hams and vivid bottles of pickles. You can buy French letters here, too, and packs of playing cards with nudes on the back, finishing with a plate of cockles, mussels or whelks. The background to all this is the castellated entrance to the Arsenal, with a mortar on each side, this device of a mortar being repeated in the engraved glass windows of the Royal Mortar public house at the corner of Woolwich New Road. Near the Royal Mortar is another relic of more spacious days – the jellied eel shop and 'noted eel pie house'. White hanging lamps bend over the green and gold fascia bearing the magic word 'Eels', a delicacy still highly esteemed in Woolwich.

The village of Charlton on the heights above Woolwich is worth visiting, if only for an interesting inn, a Victorian pub and various small haberdashers and mixed businesses. There is a sturdy Georgian church of brick with a crenellated tower and a sundial, surrounded by a crowded churchyard and shapely dark trees. In autumn, the view of the church and trees, with the Victorian drinking fountain under a conical tiled roof in the foreground, is like an early watercolour drawing in warm browns and blue-greys. Charlton House, a Jacobean mansion of brick and stone lies behind, with a triumphal arch facing the entrance across the lawn. Its semicircular drive commences with the most remarkable lavatory known to me in London, being no less than a seventeenth-century gazebo suitably converted to accommodate both sexes. Sir Adam Newton who built the house in 1607 would no doubt be greatly surprised by the transformation. Charlton House was occupied by the family and its descendants until 1915 when it became a military hospital. It was acquired by the Greenwich Borough Council in 1925, and is now a community centre, an even more pitiful fate than opening it to the *hoi polloi* at half-a-crown a head. The music of harpsichord and spinet is heard no more: one is far more likely to hear 'Knees up Mother Brown', for community singing is one of the dreadful activities encountered in such places.

St Nicholas Deptford :
Portrait of Everyman

II

The Richness of Deptford

———— ✳ ————

DEPTFORD is separated from Greenwich by Deptford Creek (we are now moving westwards along the river in the direction of the City). To the usual traveller, the kind who will not read this book, the place is uninviting. Actually there is enough richness to keep the offbeat connoisseur happy for weeks on end. The High Street has been invaded by new serve-yourself, cut price shops, all-nite laundries and chicken Barb-E-Qs, which are taking over the older properties, though bits of these are still to be seen above the flashy, new façades.

From the Catholic church, the Virgin, safe in her stone grotto overgrown with ivy, surveys the teeming working-class and coloured population, and there are walk-round bazaars of the real old sort, with clothes hanging up, carpets and overalls: fruit stalls are everywhere, at nearly every street corner, even on a week-day. There are besides good pubs for the thirsty traveller – the White Swan, for example, handsome, mid-Victorian, with a carved and coloured swan on the corner, and the Harp of Erin. Whenever I am in Deptford, I always eat at the same establishment, a working men's caff. The food there is good, rough and served in

28

generous portions. Of course, there are chips with everything – except the apple tart. This book has been almost entirely written at the plastic topped tables of these retreats, which are well supplied with ashtrays advertising Woodbines and where outsize bottles of sauce are not neglected. The patrons who have left their greasy marks on the walls are either young East End deadbeats or old men who ought to have been dead long ago. The two groups have certain things in common – a carelessness in the matter of clean linen amounting to indifference and an uncertainty in the use of knife and fork. The old men fill up football coupons.

St Paul's, Deptford, is close at hand, behind the High Street, in a beautifully kept garden. I sometimes think it the finest piece of Baroque architecture in London, St Paul's Cathedral excepted. The whole building deserves the closest study. Its interior arrangements give a remarkable sense of spaciousness; the organization and penetration of space is, of course, the main achievement of the baroque style. The plain surfaces of the great Corinthian columns and the walls are contrasted with deep mouldings on cornice and ceiling. There are views of windows through windows, the vestries on each side of the chancel having tall windows through which those of the outer wall can be seen – an intriguing, theatrical, spatial device. Smaller details to note include the pulpit, the rich organ case and a window of eighteenth-century glass. St Paul's was consecrated on 30 June 1730. Its exterior is particularly fine, with more finesse, more delicacy than Hawksmoor would have admitted. Very impressive is the porch with its monumental Roman Doric columns, ending as it abuts on the west wall in a grand rusticated pilaster, one on each side. The great lateral staircases emphasize the dramatic, theatrical feeling of the whole.

St Nicholas, Deptford, is a riverside church with seafaring associations, as might be expected from its name. Captain Edward Fenton, the companion of Frobisher, was buried here. The medieval tower was preserved when the rest of the church was rebuilt in the seventeenth century. Nothing could be more appalling than the skulls over the churchyard gate. Erosion by a couple of centuries of wind and rain has increased the realistic effect of the carving: they now appear like a pair of giants' skulls dug out of the grave, the mould still upon them: I have drawn one (opposite) and called it 'Portrait of Everyman'. Go down the street from St Nicholas's, between the flats – Deptford Green so-called – to the river. The *Golden Hind* berthed between this point and Watergate Street. Later she was permanently moored here by command of Queen Elizabeth, after she had knighted Drake on board his own ship, 'as a monument of his own and his country's glory'. The glory has now quite gone. Where the great and magnificent queen came with her retinue is the Deptford Transforming Station, patches of weed, derelict cars and old tin cans. Only the most vivid imagination is equal to the task of peopling the scene with courtiers, richly caparisoned horses, men-at-arms and all the pageantry of a state occasion. The name Armada Street, however, commemorates the association.

Watergate Street, strangely antique, is a narrow alley lined on one side by a

29

high brick wall, overhung with trees. Old cobbles of varying sizes, mostly large and uneven, still pave the entry. Walk down it on to the causeway at low tide, and admire the fine low eye level view of Greenwich from the river's edge, where the water laps softly and the mud has a salty, seagoing smell.

In my *London Nobody Knows*, I gave some impressions of the Royal Victoria Yard, Deptford, as it was when the Navy had moved out after some centuries of occupation. In only a few years, the entire site of some forty-five acres has been transformed. Great, towering blocks of flats have pushed up above the old naval buildings, and a new riverside town is fast appearing. In spite of its long and close association with the river, it is many years since Deptford had public access to the Thames. A solid wedge of industrial buildings bars the riverside off, but the new scheme is to open out the whole length of the river-front of the yard, which will then be laid out as an open space, retaining the old rum stores, Governor's quarters, the river gates and stairs (and incidentally a 1940 blockhouse to be kept as a relic) and the walled garden with its ancient mulberry tree. (Drawing of river front and eighteenth-century blocks opposite.)

However much one detests bureaucrats and planning, this scheme is certainly imaginative – eminently so; the tenants of the houses and flats will have enviable views up and down the river; the whole water front will be restored to life, with the activity of Deptford Wharf and the Surrey Docks as an ever changing spectacle to be seen for nothing from the tallest blocks. (Ships come in with timber to Deptford and return with cars and lorries on deck.) The old Pickling Dock where the masts of three-deckers were seasoned has been filled in, but the Yard from its fine entrance gates and adjoining Georgian terraces (these houses are still Admiralty property) to the river stairs is eloquent of the period of Nelson. The old sugar store has been demolished, but the fine trees have been carefully preserved. It was here that Samuel Pepys came to straighten out the muddle and maladministration in Naval affairs, to organize the fitting out of the Fleet to fight against the Dutch and, as a private perquisite, to visit Mrs Bagwell, having packed her husband safely off to sea.

On my last visit, the Yard had an air of utter desolation. Grass grew in the old cobbles, grass waist high in the old walled garden, where striped pinks flowered in solitude in overgrown borders, and sparrows, the only signs of life, quarrelled in the depths of the mulberry. On the recent occasion, I worked my way through a torn up landscape of huge, half-built blocks, cranes and excavating machines, and the caretaker, temporarily installed in one of the eighteenth-century buildings, took me round. We went over the empty Admiralty block, and I admired the old fireplaces, all, as he told me, 'comin' aht'. On the walls were remains of old official instructions – firewatching posters and similar relics of a bygone age. We went on to the roof; the day was hot and the sun shone on the river. The atmosphere was singularly clear; I could see the heights of Blackheath plainly. We talked of Drake.

'It's still called Watergate Street,' said my conductor, 'that's where Drake had

the *Golden Hind*, and he gave his cloak for Queen Elizabeth to step on. Up the street is St Nicholas's church. There used to be a lot of taverns there in the old days, and that's where that poet, Bacon, was stabbed in a brawl. And them big people in America – they wanted to come and open him up, but they wouldn't wear it, because, you see, it would have proved that Shakespeare was Marlowe and the bottom would drop out of the industry. . . . There's been a fellow painting away at the Greenwich Hospital for months. 'E was a *real* hartist. 'E 'ad a beret. It was a big pickter and 'e done it in oils.'

From the roof we could see where the foundations remained of the various demolished storehouses, the bakery for ships' biscuits and so on.

'See them foundations – they're so strong they had to be blown up last week – the prisoners built them in the Napoleonic Wars, same as they built the London prisons – Holloway.'

I also visited the rum store. The rum came in bulk, and was piped into the store and kept in vats. The channels for the pipes are still to be seen. Under the new scheme, these buildings are to be retained: they are to have their interiors re-modelled, converting them into small flats. The sheds in front of the store houses are to go, but these are of no architectural value. My guide informed me that they were first to be used as location shots for a film about Jack the Ripper, not that Jack had any connexion with Deptford.

'They're going to turn the rum store into a slaughter house and have imitation meat and a few real horses hanging about. Then Jack the Ripper is going to do the gal in. There's going to be a soup kitchen, too, all taken 'ere in the rum store, all the poor people are lying on the floor, waiting for medicines and the old Salvation Army looking after 'em.'

Film companies, British film companies at least, are addicted to riverside location shots. Another riverside area to be used for this purpose recently is Clink Street, Southwark, which blossomed out in a rash of overhanging signs to become the background for episodes in *Tom Jones*.

The mulberry still bloomed in the garden, the vine, too, in the damaged hot-house and the figs were putting forth their fruit, but the laced pinks were nowhere to be seen. I went over to the coachhouse, which still has its stables attached.

My caretaker guide said, 'The old chap who used to live here give me some pictures. "Here you are", he says, "they're pretty pictures." One was an oil, a lake scene, and the artist had scribbled his name across the corner. I said it was dirty. The old chap said, "Tea, that's what you clean them with, tea. Cold tea, no milk nor sugar, just plain tea. There's nothing like tea for cleaning pictures. All the experts use it, and they won't use nothing else".'

III

My Life in Rotherhithe

———————— * ————————

THERE was an unusually weak ebb tide on the Essex coast in the afternoon of 31 January 1953, and the flood and high tide warning which ensued was the prelude to the most vivid memory I have of Rotherhithe – the great Thames flood disaster which created havoc of stupendous proportions along the Essex coast, the river far inland and the disasters of Canvey Island.

The defensive walls of the Thames stretch from Essex to the Pool of London and include wharves, quays, plateaux of higher ground made up from refuse dumps on the marshes and the old embankments of the river which date from an early period. But there have been occasions, the most recent being in 1928 and 1953, when the Thames, always seeking to encroach on the marshland of Essex, helped by moon, sun and wind, makes short work of man-made obstacles, once indeed, in February 1736, overflowing into Westminster Hall to a height of a couple of feet.

The coming of the railways, the building of the docks and subsequent mushrooming of towns round them – such as Silvertown, Canning Town, East Ham and Tilbury – led to the nearer Thames-side marshlands being solidified and protected to a greater extent than ever before, but the outlying marshlands remained very vulnerable.

Although the gales over the whole country had been extraordinary at that time, there seemed nothing unusual that Saturday evening in 1953, though the river seemed to be somewhat swollen and the wind was very strong. In fact, although I did not know it, the inundations had already started along the Essex coast and, as for the tide, it was fully six foot higher than had been predicted. I was awakened in the small hours of Sunday by the wailing of police sirens in Rotherhithe Street. I got up and dressed and found the entire street awake. My neighbours were removing furniture from their downstairs rooms. I decided that my house, being higher than the rest, might escape, and therefore I took no such precautions; in this I was proved right, though the water rose half-way up the windows at the back of the house overlooking the river. Luckily they held; only a thin trickle of water infiltrated. Looking out of those rear windows was like looking into an aquarium.

The other houses in Rotherhithe Street were lower, and as I went outside, a great semicircular wave came over the bombed land between the Angel and the row in which I lived and raced across the street like a tidal wave. The ground floors

ROTHERHITHE AWASH – the great Flood Feb 1953

of all the houses except mine were awash immediately, the whole situation being rendered very eerie by the darkness, the velocity of the wind and the noises from the black and swollen river. Barges, moored below the houses, were now level with the gutters. Farther along Rotherhithe Street, the river poured over at all the stairs and entries, bringing timber, chairs and other material with it. When I had light enough, I made the drawing. It shows the Thames flowing all round the Angel public house in the foreground, instead of well below its balcony as usual. In the early light, the scene appeared desolate in the extreme. The buildings along the Redriff shore appeared to grow out of the water in the manner of Venetian palaces, and the extraordinary height of the shipping added fantasy to melancholy. Rotherhithe was thoroughly inundated, and I could not help thinking of the lines in Jean Ingelow's poem:

And all the world was in the sea.

But the nightmare of Canvey Island was still being told.

34

MY LIFE IN ROTHERHITHE

In Central London the river behaved in less unruly fashion; still, even there – in Chelsea, for instance – it rose to the very top of the Embankment parapet. With us, in Rotherhithe, its effects were felt for days, for the streets were black with evil smelling mud for a long time, and all along the riverside ways from Rotherhithe to Greenwich one encountered flotsam and jetsam in strange, unexpected places – visiting cards left by the great and hostile tide.

The river walk from the Angel – or from farther west – Tower Bridge or London Bridge even – to Deptford is one of the most interesting in London. All along the river are points of access, though not so many as in former years. You can start at St Saviour's Dock, one of the smallest and most ancient, once the property of Bermondsey Abbey, near where Jacob's Island used to be, and work your way past a variety of intriguingly named stairs, by narrow ways smelling of merchandise, below great warehouses. After St Saviour's Dock comes Fountain Stairs, followed by Cherry Garden Pier (drawing from Cherry Garden Pier looking east to Rotherhithe Church below), which forms a sort of floating observation platform from which (with permission) you can have some of the most stimulating views of the Lower Pool. Pepys came to Cherry Garden; in his day Rotherhithe was rural to a degree unbelievable now. No trace of the Cherry Garden remains; the last old houses, which included a dairy, have only recently disappeared. Going east along the river from Cherry Garden are Platform Stairs, King's Stairs, Prince's Stairs and Elephant Stairs just short of St Mary's Church. Next come Church Stairs, Hanover Stairs and Globe and Pageants Stairs as the river bends to the Canada, Albion, Greenland, Russia and Lavender Docks.

The best time to see the river from Cherry Garden Pier is at high tide on a week-day, especially if a freshening breeze makes the water choppy. Cranes are whirling cargoes from the holds of steamers, barges are being towed by ubiquitous tugs – the whole river comes to life. Turn towards Tower Bridge and see the new sky line of the City above the Pool of London – a dreary prospect, only made tolerable by the architecture of earlier periods – St Paul's, the Monument, the City churches and Tower Bridge itself. I have not drawn Tower Bridge, my near neighbour for many years, in this book, except incidentally. Everyone knows it well enough by now, but I am not sure whether it or the skill with which Sir Horace Jones, the architect, solved the problem of giving massiveness without coarseness to Gothic forms is appreciated sufficiently.

Where my house used to be is now an empty space. Memory is so fickle that it now requires an effort to recall that picturesque assembly of old houses with the Jolly Waterman in the middle and mine, the Little Midshipman, at the far end and the barge building down below. However, I made a drawing of the Jolly Waterman from the river, with the barges floating above and a welder at work, and I reproduce it opposite as a record of departed things. The shore of Wapping, with Wapping Old Stairs, the River Police station and the Flemish-like church tower above a grey border of warehouses, could be seen from the bay window of the Little Midshipman. There were early mornings when the river at low tide was as undisturbed as a woodland pool, and the sun, rising through vapour as it does in Turner's painting, touched fleecy clouds with a warm, peach light and out of the blue mist regilded the metalwork on Tower Bridge, the fire-ball on the Monument and the vanes of churches with a transient gold. Sometimes there were sunsets that turned the river into liquid fire, burning over the cobalt blue distance beyond Tower Bridge, and winter storms, whipping the Thames into pounding waves, were made especially dramatic when lightning flashed from a green and purple sky. There were those evenings when velvety darks veiled the river after a hot summer day, and, in the fading light, the *Royal Sovereign* made her way back to Tower Pier, a floating Derby Day, crammed with Cockneys. They had dared the perils of the river in the morning – Grandpa, Uncle Joe, Aunt Florrie, the kids, Ron and Mavis, and all the rest of them – had loaded themselves to the Plimsoll line with beer, candy floss and shell fish, and were celebrating their safe return from Southend with music and song, which floated across the river. The ship glided effortlessly in mid-stream, and the lights of her lower decks were reflected in the rippling water.

PYTHON

'Few European cities,' says Henry James, 'have a finer river than the Thames, but none certainly has expended more ingenuity in producing a sordid river-front. For miles and miles you see nothing but the sooty backs of warehouses, or perhaps they are sooty faces: in buildings so utterly expressionless it is impossible to distinguish. They stand massed together on the banks of the wide, turbid stream . . . a damp-looking dirty blackness is the universal tone.'

In contrast, we have Whistler's poetic description of the riverside at dusk, when these same poor buildings become palaces in the night, the chimneys campanile under the influences of evening mist. It was in Rotherhithe, Wapping, Shadwell and similarly unprepossessing, industrialized reaches of the river that Whistler found those subjects for his exquisite Thames set of etchings, begun in 1859. In these, Whistler exploited the beauty of warehouses, barges and the patterns of mast and rigging at a time when such subjects were considered unpictorial; only Turner had had an insight into their possibilities. These early etchings are remarkable for delicacy of draughtsmanship, dwelling as they do on the textures of tile, timber, brickwork and the involved detail of waterside building. These and the paintings produced at this period, 'The Thames in Ice', the 'Demolition of Old Westminster Bridge' (actually the striking of the scaffolding from the new bridge) and the painting called 'Wapping' comprise a more factual aspect of Whistler's work: the later Nocturnes, dreamed out of the river mist and the fireworks at Cremorne, represent the river from an entirely different approach. Both are immensely valuable to lovers of the Thames. 'Wapping' is very eloquent of the river at this wonderful time; Legros, afterwards Slade Professor, sits on a balcony (presumably that of the pub where Whistler stayed during this Thames period) with the artist's mistress, Jo, a somewhat wooden figure in the foreground; behind is a complex panorama of sailing boats, paddle tugs, dinghies and riverside architecture.

The walk along the Thames continues along Rotherhithe Street by Elephant Lane, between the grey warehouses, dusty with deposits of flour. There is tremendous activity at high tide, and the speed at which the barges are unloaded is equalled by the vigour of the oaths of the lightermen. My drawing was made from Archers Wharf where some 250 tons of Canadian flour are unloaded daily. The men in the barges wear knitted caps; flour sticks to their eyebrows and eyelashes, giving them a clown-like appearance. Their language, rich in four letter words, is largely about racing losses, but the pigeons who are constant visitors on these wharves are sublimely indifferent; only the ships' hooters affect them, and, when these are let off, the birds start from the barges in flocks of several hundred.

When I lived in Rotherhithe, my life for a time was made miserable in the early mornings when the tide was low by the horror of pigeon shooting by a blackguard who maimed, and left to die, as many as he actually killed. The R.S.P.C.A. and the River Police put an end to his visits, I am glad to record, but had I been

able to get hold of his gun, as I tried to, I should have made no difficulty about turning it on him myself.

Not far from Archers Wharf is the masons' yard and the wharf where marble, granite and serpentine (tricky material to handle) are unloaded and where the blocks are worked. On the other side of the street is one of the most fascinating relics of the river, all that remains of the old engine house and shaft of Brunel's tunnel on the Rotherhithe side. On the Wapping side, the shaft is actually the

ST MARY Rotherhithe

DANC
OVERS
HOIST

SJ Fletcher

Underground station, and the wooden staircases and their iron handrailings are the originals. But at Rotherhithe the shaft was by-passed when the Thames Tunnel had railway metals laid in it and the Rotherhithe Station built a short distance from it. This shaft was the first to be sunk and, like the Tunnel as a whole, was a triumph of engineering skill over incredible obstacles. Only part of it remains above ground, fenced off to prevent children from dropping into the depths below. The shaft has a classic cornice, the whole being of brick covered with pinky yellow Roman cement rendering.

The old pump house is now used for cutting inscriptions on grave stones. Crated blocks of granite, tombstone-shaped but awaiting inscription, and odds and ends of marble fill the yard. As I wandered round on my last visit, an old man, a facsimile of the White Knight in *Through the Looking Glass*, was passing water against a half-finished memorial. From this ancient, after this launching ceremony was over, I got interesting reminiscences of Rotherhithe at the turn of the century, when local life was much closer knit, though infinitely poorer than it is now, and when the parishioners of St Mary's turned up in their Sunday best (including the occasional top hat) to church on Christening Sunday. He remembered when the area around the shaft was planted out with trees, and told me that if I cared to look among the debris, I should find some of their stumps, which I found to be the case.

Near the yard is the small riverside pub known in my Rotherhithe days as the Spread Eagle, but rechristened some years ago as the Mayflower, part of a P.R.-man's publicity brainwave in connexion with the replica of the *Mayflower*. The pub is small and interesting, and a curiosity of its licence is that postage stamps are sold there, besides booze, a facility originally intended for seamen. It was used by Brunel's men during the tunnelling works.

This part of the riverside walk is full of interest. St Mary's Church (the drawing of it from the Spread Eagle pub is on pages 40–41) and churchyard garden is particularly satisfactory, a green and pleasant enclave among miles of warehouses. You come upon it quite suddenly, without warning, and, even when you are used to it, the pleasure of encounter never stales. The playground by the church usually has a handful of children playing there; this juxtaposition of noisy, everyday life and the mariners – some from the Mayflower – waiting in their graves for their Pilot to come on board gives one ample material for thought, while the river runs swiftly, like Time itself. After the tunnel shaft, Rotherhithe Street gets dull for a time, with nothing but flat-faced warehouses and grim blocks of 1930-type flats, but there is a good open view of the Prospect of Whitby (only its riverside exterior is of architectural merit nowadays) and Shadwell Church from the swing bridge at the entrance to the Surrey Commercial Dock.

Farther along is Horseferry Wharf, from which I made the inset drawing of the small Dutch cargo boat. I used to have these Dutch boats anchor beneath my house at one time, usually with a Keeshond, a Dutch barge dog, on board. The Dutch sailors were amusing themselves as I drew by fishing for driftwood with boathooks and a ladder and quacking at the Thames ducks who swam under the stern to cadge scraps of food. Such incidents are readily absorbed by the passengers of pleasure boats, the present day descendants of the penny steamers, on the trip to Greenwich. It is amusing to see the passengers' heads swivel first to this side now to that as the man with the microphone feeds them with tasty scraps of information. Once, when taking my mother for this trip, I was astounded by the wildly inaccurate details, and so, when he appeared at Greenwich with his little money bag, I said to her, 'Everything he said was all wrong. I never heard such rubbish, and I'm not paying for such stuff.'

'Oh yes, you must,' was her firm rejoinder. 'He may not know anything about it, but he did his best.' And on that quixotic note, I paid up.

After 59 Rotherhithe Street had been christened 'The Little Midshipman', for no other reason than an enthusiasm for *Dombey and Son*, I was often amused to hear from across the water '. . . over there on your right' (eyes right from the rubber necks) 'is Dickens's own genuine "Little Midshipman", where he used to stay . . .' And once, on Waterloo Bridge, I heard the cornerman tell his passengers, much to my satisfaction if not to theirs, 'we are about to pass the Temple Gardens where the first shots were fired in the Wars of the Roses.' This I consider a gem, a diamond as big as the Ritz.

Some of these pleasure boats, especially when their awnings are up, are quite period, but none could surpass the *Princess Beatrice*. She was built in 1896 in the yard opposite Tagg's Island, and had polished brasswork, fluted columns and engraved glass – the most delightful of the surviving Thames built steamers. She sank at Richmond in March 1964, after breaking from her moorings at Eel Pie Island, a melancholy end. Her great days were in the Edwardian period when she carried racing parties from Molesey Lock to Hurst Park.

On the river opposite Horseferry Wharf is the refuse plant of Stepney Borough Council. Huge hoppers slide the rubbish of several thousands of dustbins into barges waiting below. The rubbish is then towed off by tugs to be dumped down river – but still the loaded lorries come. Once, when I was mooning about there, the dustmen found a toy yacht in the ashes and launched it in the river – a *Marie Celeste* in miniature.

Next along the river walk comes another of those architectural surprises, kept in readiness, as it were, for lovers of London – the remarkably well-preserved Nelson House, undoubtedly a Georgian merchant's residence, and now used as a firm's office at the Nelson Dry Dock. There were several such houses in Rotherhithe until comparatively recent years, relics of its prosperous days when wealthy merchants and plantation and ship owners lived where they directed their operations, on Thames-side. The house is separated from the road by a brick wall and an iron garden gate. It has a Roman Doric porch up a flight of steps, with a three-light window above – a fine old house of yellow brick entirely surrounded by commercial buildings.

At this point, take an 82 bus – on top, for the grandstand view of the vast Surrey Docks, water, timber boats from the Baltic and timber stacked on all sides – to Lower Road, Deptford. And on the way back to London, note the caryatid figures, once part of the vanished Assembly Hall, opposite St Olave's Hospital, Rotherhithe, as the road bends towards the Rotherhithe Tunnel. The ladies have had little to do since the place was destroyed by bombs. They merely hold up a bit of cornice and give moral support to the posters. These classic dames remind me of those of the Erectheum, copied in the porch of St Pancras Church but, instead of gazing out over the ruins of Athens or over the Euston Road, they content themselves by watching the buses going down to Catford and the ambulances arriving at the hospital gates.

IV

Week-end in Wapping

—— * ——

WE could walk through the Rotherhithe Tunnel (after inspecting the lavatory, which has notices in Norwegian as well as English, opposite the Norwegian church) but it is a deafening, stinking experience, and you emerge, though well on the way to Limehouse, three parts choked with the exhaust fumes of lorries. Therefore, we will take the Underground through Brunel's tunnel, a mushroom-smelling, claustrophobic experience, hoping, as I always do, that after so many years the whole affair will not spring a leak and feeling glad the drivers race like mad through the dark. At Wapping never go up by the lift, for by so doing you lose the opportunity of seeing Brunel's work from the inside. Look up the shaft from a point about three-quarters of the way down, admire the great stone cornice and the sweep of the giant cylinder above you, and inhale the spicy smells drifting in from the warehouses, mingling with the damp, mouldy tang of the tunnel.

Either way, east or west, from the station are innumerable opportunities for riverside exploration. A westward course will take you to the Wapping Police Station and Wapping Old Stairs:

> Your Polly has never been faithless, she swears,
> Since last year we parted on Wapping Old Stairs.

Next to the stairs was Execution Dock, where sailors and others convicted for criminal offences on the Thames were strung on the gallows.

Polly, faithful or not, was here in great numbers up to the mid-nineteenth century. According to Frank Harris, Ruskin, who was Turner's executor, discovered a number of bawdy paintings of riverside tarts done by Turner on his visits to Wapping and destroyed them. It is certain that Turner did produce something of the kind, done when his mind was giving way and, therefore, not adding appreciably to his artistic achievement. If Harris's version is to be accepted, these destroyed paintings were of the private parts of prostitutes: it is hard to come to any definite conclusion on the matter. Turner is known to have visited Wapping at regular intervals in sailor's garb, if the legend has any truth in it. On the other hand, he had property there, which he would most certainly manage for himself. Who can tell?

45

The Wapping Police Station is slightly *art nouveau* in design. Dickens was a frequent visitor to its predecessor on the same site and records, in one or two of his occasional papers, its atmosphere in that time of rowing boats, dark lanterns, sailing ships and Gaffer Hexams. The Thames division evolved from the private force established by the West India Company to protect their cargoes against the extensive pilfering of Thames-side before the coming of the Docks. A scheme for policing the river, which directly resulted in the formation of a Marine Police Force, was introduced by a Dr Patrick Colquhoun in collaboration with Jeremy Bentham, and the first office, on the site of the present Divisional Headquarters at Wapping, was opened in 1798.

Bentham, who was something of a mummy long before he attained his present status of actually being one, boxed up in University College, would be surprised at the organization which has evolved from that old police force, largely recruited from the seamen and watermen. They had to be strong, tough types, capable of dealing with the violent ruffians of the waterfront. Nearly one third of the port workers handling cargoes were known to be thieves or receivers; the whole river-side population was concerned in organized plundering, and at least half of all the cargoes entering the port disappeared in this way. The efforts of this early police force were in time successful in breaking up these gangs, and the construction of the first docks put an end to discharging and loading on the open river, where pilfering was easy, especially by night.

In the early days, the work of the Thames Division was carried out by means of rowing boats and sailing craft. Vivid descriptions of these water borne Peelers were written by Dickens. In them, we get a picture of hard-boiled characters gliding about in the shadow of the great sailing ships, ears and eyes alerted for unusual sounds and sights, on the look out for water rats – the various kinds of river thieves variously classed as Tier-Rangers (the felons who burgled boats instead of houses), the Lumpers (lightermen, who, while unloading cargo, loaded selected portions, tobacco and spirits mainly, into concealed pockets), Truckers (or smugglers) and other nefarious types dedicated to the art of pinching.

Motor-boats were introduced in 1910, and today there are over thirty duty boats, all maintained at the Wapping workshops. The police stations were originally hulks, but these have now been replaced by buildings ashore, with the exception of Waterloo Pier, which is housed on a pontoon. This remains unique as the only floating police station; one of the rarer sights of London is to see this water-borne cop-shop towed away by a launch to Tilbury, as it is at periodic intervals, for an overhaul with its complement of coppers on board. Thames Division covers about thirty-six miles, from Teddington Lock to Dartford Creek; the system of beats and patrols is similar to that carried out on shore but, in addition to protecting property on ships and barges and on the wharves and riverside, the Thames Police also deal with collisions, fires, salvage, accidents and suicides. A fair number of dead bodies are recovered from the river each year, and many others, both those who have fallen into the river by accident and those who have gone in deliberately, are rescued – an arrangement which would have put Rogue Rider-hood, who made his living by plundering the bodies floating on the tide at Lime-house, clean out of business.

This riverside walk from Wapping to Tower Hill is one of absolute peace at week-ends, Sunday especially. It may be that life on the lower river is going on, but there is little sign or sound of it. The wharves, warehouses, cranes and derricks stand in a Sabbath silence; the lightermen and bargees have left them to the gulls, and the river laps softly against its deserted quays in a temporary return to its ancient peace. Now and again you see a policeman on his beat; his 'good after-noon, sir' sounds odd in the silent street, as if you and he were the last men on earth but still preserved the old relationships and formalities. Otherwise, the silence is unbroken, except for the sound of city clocks and bells and the hollow echo of your feet on the granite setts. The solitary riverside wayfarer can revel in the luxury of being separated from his importunate fellows, for the wicked cease from troubling in Wapping at week-end. He is a freeman of an almost entirely deserted city; his subjects are only the sparrows quibbling in the horse droppings still found here, picking, as it were, crumbs from the rich man's stable. You can meditate on the different character of the Thames as you walk – on its upper reaches, with its punts and parasols, straw boaters and blazers among the scented rushes and meadow sweet – and contrast it with Wapping, a place of articulated lorries, overalls, sacks, mud and spice. Or you can ponder on the treasures fished out of the river bed and foreshore for many years, relics from the Bronze Age, swords and spears the Romans carelessly left in the river, statues, coins, pottery from the Middle Ages; the river is an avid, if indiscriminating, collector of every-thing from heads of Roman deities to detergent bottles, and is at present especially interested in old prams and bicycle frames.

The late Georgian architecture of Wapping Pier Head is worth stopping to examine. Note the royal coat of arms and the ragwort and other weeds flourishing among the bollards. In an atmosphere of melancholy, there is the old churchyard of St John of Wapping, the church tower itself, designed by Joel Johnson, and the ruined schoolhouse, slowly disintegrating for want of attention. Years ago, I remember how the churchyard looked in the summer; there was a fine old gate, solid eighteenth-century stuff made, like the church, for the use of substantial mariners, and through it (it was invariably closed) you could see the old tomb-stones, half hidden by grass, in the shadows of lilacs and laburnums.

I have always been very fond of Wapping, and used to go there to loiter and moon about several times each week when I was a student at the Slade – a pro-ceeding I much preferred to drawing or painting nudes or painting portraits of dim old men. Once, long before I lived on the river myself, I asked a young Bobbie if he knew of anywhere to buy or rent. I told him I loved the area and had composed a pastiche of a Victorian ballad on it (the words I have now forgotten, but the insidious tune I composed is still unfortunately in memory). I told him there were thousands living in places like Dorking or Penge who hated every day of their existence and longed to get out of it all and go native in Wapping. He refused to believe it. As to the ballad, he couldn't say as there was no accounting for tastes, but what he did know was this: any man who wanted to live in this Gawdforsaken hole was stark, staring bonkers, and that's all there was to it.

The pubs in the area call for no special mention, except to regret the disappearance of the Turk's Head before the war, but the Town of Ramsgate is one that cannot be overlooked when the occasion is ripe for a snack, a glass of ale and a snug bar in which to have them. There are slums on the north side yet, but the rural character of the district as it was some centuries ago (Wapping was one of the first East End districts to be built up and settled by seafaring men and those who supplied them) is indicated by street names such as Hermitage Wall.

Wapping was one of the centres of the curious dishonest trade of making wooden nutmegs at a time when the real article was a highly prized expensive commodity.

All the way along to St Katherine's Way, warehouse walls rise up like cliffs of yellow brick, with glimpses of ships seen through archways and, on working days, men loading and unloading barges. There is an interesting group of small warehouses by Alderman Stairs, one being of the eighteenth century, and then, after a few more twists and windings, you come upon the delightful Dockmaster's Office – Georgian, of grey brick with green painted woodwork; lawns and bollards are laid out in the space in front and a white cat (definitely on the establishment) peers at the river from behind the lace-curtained windows. The whole scheme is a charming example of that homely classical architecture associated with the English canals and the smaller customs houses. It forms a framework for a dramatic view of Tower Bridge, which must be the grandest gate to any port in the world: the Victorians were always at their best in engineering architecture, especially when they had to find an answer to new problems.

Tower Hill is, or was, a London village, with its own church. Traces of this remain yet. Once, in the company of the Rev Tubby Clayton and his Cairn terrier (who brought along a squeaky Mickey Mouse), I toured the whole area, my guide energetically expressing his disgust at the demolition of the old houses on the West side, sloping down to the Tiger public house and the river, and the horrible new blocks then about to replace them. Old-fashioned family concerns who had traded on Tower Hill for generations were, he said, forced to clear out or be accommodated in air-conditioned offices entirely unsuitable for them. At that time, the old building on the corner of Mark Lane was still intact and in the possession of John Martin's, the wine shippers. Its interest was in what had originally been an inner courtyard, paved with Tudor bricks in a herring-bone pattern and built over at various later periods, the courtyard paving remaining as the floor of several store rooms. Here the merchant ships of England were organized to fight

Dockmaster's Office
St Katharine's Dock

the Spaniards and the defences against the Armada planned. Today a Post Office occupies the site. Last of all, we studied the church – Tubby Clayton's church – in detail, and he showed me the place in the crypt set apart for the ashes of members of Toc H.

'Death is a fearful thing,' I said, 'but nothing makes it more so than the practice of cremation. . . . What about the Resurrection?' Nothing more was said on the matter. When we got outside, I was right glad to hear the squeaky Mickey Mouse.

Waves of rubbernecks pour out from the tube on Tower Hill in the summer, or they are decanted by the thousand from glass-roofed coaches. Once on dry land, they stare round them like automatons. A dozen ice-cream vans – none of the ones with barley sugar columns and pictures of waterfalls and roses on them, such as there were when I was a schoolboy in the 'thirties, but up to the minute concerns – sell hokey-pokey by the ton. The sun beats down: I hope it will not melt the visitors' heads. Everyone has dark glasses, cameras and ice-cream cornets. There is a rush for fruit. Some of the visitors even go round the church – they are so keen to see everything. New waves of bums pour off the river boats. All have one thing in view, the Tower. In this book, we will, I think, allow them to enjoy it in peace. However, history is still being manufactured here; witness the ceremony when Sir Winston Churchill left Tower Pier for the last time on that January day when the pipers played the wild music of 'The Flowers of the Forest' and the lowered jibs of the cranes on Hay's Wharf paid their own strange final tribute.

Turn east from Wapping Tube Station, and you have in front of you the great

East End, stretching north to Bethnal Green, Hackney and Clapton and on your right to Shadwell, Limehouse, Poplar, Blackwall . . . farther still, if you have a mind for it. The road turns to Shadwell Church at the Prospect of Whitby, where I used to lunch in my student days, cheaply and agreeably in what was then an unsophisticated, unspoiled riverside tavern. An old woman like a figure by Nicholas Maes peeled potatoes in a back room, and you could wander round and amuse yourself with the bric-à-brac left by sailors while waiting for your meal. The pub takes its curious name from the Whitby colliers which, in former times, were moored on this part of the river. The basin below Shadwell church was where Dickens went on board the Mormon emigrant ship, the *Amazon* (finding contrary to his expectations, everything shipshape and Bristol fashion) bound for the Great Salt Lake. This part of the East End has been recorded in detail by Dickens, with his usual gusto and instinct for the telling phrase. He describes visits to the sailors' dancing and drinking dens in the region of the Ratcliffe Highway.

'Down by the Docks,' he says, 'they "board seamen" at the eating-houses, the public-houses, the slop-shops, the coffee shops, the tally shops . . . board them, as it were, in the piratical sense, making them bleed terribly and giving no quarter . . . You may hear the Incomparable Joe Jackson sing the Standard of England, with a horn pipe, any night, or any day may see at the waxwork, for a penny and no waiting, him as killed the policeman at Acton and suffered for it.' ·

Today the entire quarter has got sobered down and altered out of all recognition. There are few drunks and fewer sailors, with or without hornpipes. Malays and Chinese have gone glimmering, and the children of Israel no longer sell pewter watches in gloomy, rotting slop-shops. The loose living, poxy daughters of Britannia have ceased to roam the streets; special knowledge is needed to locate them; though you will find them on summer evenings in Swedenborg Square waiting for the black men to pick them up and drive them off in outsized cars. Boys from Shadwell have gained entrance scholarships to universities. In a word, you could take your grandmother round here, even if she were one of the Plymouth Brethren.

It is the same with the pubs by the Albert Dock; they were once full of drunken, singing sailors and prostitutes, Mercantile Jack and Nancy, once again. Now they are all quiet and comfortable, go in for small jazz groups, attract West Enders who have a fancy for East End and Limehouse nights, and put up good luncheons for local business men. It must be nearly twenty years since I saw a fight between two drunken prostitutes in a pub – and even that was at the Elephant. It is depressing to think that the English once conquered half the world then got a bad conscience about it and turned respectable.

The road winds more or less by the river, past where the great Jamrack, wild beast importer, had his menagerie, over the Limehouse Cut and then into Narrow Street. These eighteenth-century houses (opposite) are the last of the old river-

51

side dwellings around here and are to be restored, having recently been reprieved from demolition. Some, as I remember, when ships' chandlers and riverside families lived in them, have charming panelled rooms. Barge repairing is still carried on here, and the place is much more marine and lively than Wapping. The old houses edge the river as they did in Whistler's day, though fewer in number, and my drawing of them and the barges below shows how interesting the water-front still is. But if you want to know what it was like in its great period, there is an etching of the late 1870s hung in the Grapes, showing the truly picturesque assembly of old houses inhabited by ships' plumbers, block and tackle makers and the like. One of these, the delightful, bow-windowed Harbourmaster's House was demolished in 1923.

I was always down in Wapping and Limehouse in 1945 and 1946, painting on the river and, though I have no idea of what became of the things I did, I made some extensive notes which have now a certain period interest.

'The bar of the Prospect of Whitby', I wrote, 'is small and dark and packed full of French sailors and women. There are ancient settles and a flagged floor; the back of the bar is hung with relics, emblems and stuffed crocodiles; also two parrots (not stuffed) in cages. . . . We sat by a roaring fire, and the landlord saw us out at closing time (I have no doubt he was glad to rid himself of us). . . . At Limehouse, the young publican, Higgins, whose family have kept the place for years, let us down on to the shore by a side passage, where we climbed on to the barges and began work. A fellow fed seagulls from a back window – a squealing, whirling cloud, dipping for an instant on the water for the bread. The back of the Grapes on the water remains as it did when Dickens described it under the name of 'The Three Jolly Fellowship Porters' in *Our Mutual Friend*. . . . I worked well until dusk, and then crossed by a precarious bridge of planks to the offices of Etheridges, where a man called Pat, who lives with his wife above, invited us to thaw out over tea and biscuits. He said that Limehouse is far tamer now than in his youth, when there were constant fights between gangs, and told of a fellow falling off a barge in the early morning and his screaming as he drowned, being caught in the underwater chains.'

These persons found drowned provided, as I have said, the livelihood for Rogue Riderhood who hung out in Limehouse Hole, an unsavoury spot now occupied by Aberdeen Wharf. Dickens was often in Limehouse in the early 1860s while at work on *Our Mutual Friend*; in fact, his godfather, a naval man, lived not far from the church. Miss Abbey Potterson, who kept the Fellowship Porters, would have no difficulty in recognizing her pub today; the bar has been made more comfortable and now includes a telly (a feature Miss Potterson would throw into the river), but its homely local flavour remains. It has an early morning licence – 6 to 8 a.m. for dockers. True, the rear room overlooking the river has been dubbed 'The Dickens Room', but its arrangements are simple enough; the temptation to cram it with Dickens relics must have been considerable.

WJ WOODWARD FISHER L

MARTIAL

Limehouse
Water front

The river view from the Grapes is not so good as that from the Prospect of Whitby. It is less interesting architecturally, being obscured on the right by the power station and in front by a fringe of wharves and chimneys, dull stuff. The interest is in the barge building below and the river traffic at high tide (drawing over the page). But where the river abruptly bends to the south to curve round the peninsula called the Isle of Dogs, the riverscape is more lively: Greenwich is in the distant bend of the river, and there are times when a sudden feeling of the wealth and vastness of London, of the magnificent scale on which it conducts its affairs (even in these mouldy days) comes over you, standing there on the balcony, with the sun on the water and the river traffic on the full tide.

A Thames sailing barge is a sight seldom seen on the river nowadays. Nothing is more symbolic of their passing than the disposal by Coubro and Scrutton of their old sailmaking premises, where sails were made until recently, in the West India Dock Road. It was built in 1860, and the cast iron railings include miniature ships' anchors at the entrance by the steps, the top of the railings being in the form of a length of rope. The Thames was alive with sailing ships and barges at the time the building was erected; now the appearance of a sailing barge is as unusual as a horse-drawn cab in the London streets. Coubro and Scrutton, now in an extensive way of business in Millwall, Tilbury and elsewhere began in Narrow Street, Limehouse (drawing opposite) as sailmakers and ships' chandlers, supplying the *Cutty Sark*, one of the fastest sailing ships ever built, and many of the China clippers. After the removal of the firm's engineering works to Millwall, the premises in the West India Dock Road – curiously reminiscent of a non-conformist chapel – were mainly used for canvas work and rigging; sailing ships were still being catered for up to and including the Great War, on occasions the firm re-rigging the ships throughout, including masts and sails.

The Isle of Dogs once had the richest soil in the London area. Its pasture lands were used for fattening sheep and cattle. As to the dogs, there are conflicting theories: no one really seems to know. It is worth a visit, if only to the Waterman's Arms, for its entertainment and collection of music hall relics. The pub itself is early-Victorian, but with a Regency, waterfront flavour. Close to it is the magnificent view of the Greenwich shore from the public garden. Though the architecture of the Isle of Dogs is mainly that of factories and docks, the streets are much cleaner than those in other parts of the East End. The terraces of small houses mostly end in little newsagents, grocers or chip shops. In fact, the fish and chips of the Isle of Dogs are fully equal to those of Lancashire, where the delicacy is at its best, and you can eat in the street out of newspaper as you walk round the island and wash the whole lot down at the Waterman's Arms. But its great feature is the never ending panorama of the river – the big ships, the tug boats, the little ships and the strings of barges seen from the riverside garden under the trees as the sun goes down and the lights come on in the hospital and along the Greenwich waterfront.

There are other pubs in the dock area worth visiting. These include the Star of the East (Victorian Italian Gothic), opposite Limehouse Church, the Pride of the Isles in Havannah Street, a genuine East End local, where people go to enjoy themselves, the Custom House Hotel in the Victoria Dock Road, interesting both architecturally and from its noisy, lively clients – mainly seamen and dockyard workers, the Tidal Basin Tavern, also near the Royal Victoria Dock, and the Gun Tavern, another pub with a seafaring atmosphere, in Poplar.

SOLE 47

BLOT

The River from
Duke Shore Wharf

V

Exploring Bankside

———— ✳ ————

FEW THINGS, I think, could be more characteristic of the apathy of modern Londoners than their failure to protest against the proposal to demolish London Bridge and to replace it by a prestressed concrete affair equal in nastiness to Waterloo Bridge. Hardly a protest was made as far as I could make out; no demands to know why the settlement could not be corrected by underpinning or, if not, why a replica could not be built – nothing but a mute acceptance. Of course, the present bridge is inadequate for traffic – it is always traffic – the traffic that at first slowly and now rapidly is eating London away, all to no purpose. The difference between the present-day apathy and the outcry when the demolition of the old Waterloo Bridge was announced is an index of the impotence and weariness of Englishmen, especially Londoners.

Needless to say, one of the London newspapers announced the scheme by the headline 'London Bridge is falling down'. This fatuous jocularity undoubtedly helps to condition the reactions of the ordinary man – makes the thing seem less outrageous to him and gets him on the way to acceptance. Whether the destruction be of bridges or liberties makes no matter, the evil is always wrapped up in a cocoon of cosiness and fun for the tame little eunuch who goes to the suburbs as the little man – Strube's little man – who has had his brain drained off for years and has now no more backbone than a jellybaby. These infantile headlines always bring out the savage in me. Were I an editor, I should scorn to assist the Establishment, the bureaucrats, in whatever they schemed or help in any way to soften the heads of readers. Such propaganda was at its most sickening during the war – London could always take it – always laughed and was cheerful when the vegetable marrow on the air raid shelter emerged unscathed from a night's bombing. One can hardly believe that such propaganda is addressed to reasoning men and women: not that it matters for they are reduced to the condition of cattle to be slaughtered anyway, and can and will do nothing if the whole of London is turned into a hell. They are allowed the luxury of grumbling and that surely is enough?

Herbert Morrison left a dreary monument to his presumption – the new Waterloo Bridge – saving, however, his greatest impertinence to the last – his ashes tipped into the Thames. A bridge should never be an unbroken horizontal on top, a curve, however subtle, being necessary for optical effect. All our great bridge builders recognized this. The present London Bridge has a monumental quality, a severe Piranesi-like grandeur about it; nothing we can ever do will compensate for its loss, except a plain, straightforward replica. We have no English architecture worth the name today, and there is no point in pretending otherwise.

The only thing to be said about Waterloo Bridge is that the poverty of its surroundings at both ends means it does no harm in its vicinity, except to Somerset House, but it adversely affects many otherwise fine views of the river. Note, too, the miserable metalwork on the parapet of the bridge (it is typical of what is done today) and compare it with the classical lamps (cast from cannon captured at Waterloo) on London Bridge.

My two drawings of London Bridge – one from Nancy's steps (over the page) and the other from a point below the Fishmongers' Hall (opposite) – will, I hope, give a notion of what future generations will miss. The present bridge was built by

London Bridge from
Nancy's Steps

Sir John Rennie and his son in 1823–31 and widened in 1904, and cost £506,000. It was opened by King William IV with much ceremony, including a Royal procession by water, a balloon ascent and a banquet on the bridge.

Our apathy may be contrasted with the consternation of the aboriginal inhabitants of Scotland Yard (wharfingers, mainly, who dealt in coal) as described by Dickens. Nobody there doubted 'that if the Lord Mayor contemplated any such dark design, he would just be clapped up in the Tower for a week or two, and then killed off for high treason'. The water in the Thames would run off, they said, but the first stone was laid, the years passed and the bridge was opened by the king himself, and this blow to the prophetic powers of the coal heavers brought about the gradual dissolution of the yard and marked the advance of civilization and change.

There has been a bridge across the Thames at or near London Bridge for over a thousand years. The Ancient Britons almost certainly had a bridge there, before the Romans came. But the most famous London Bridge was of stone (unlike its predecessors, which were of wood). A monk, Peter of Colechurch, began it in 1176. It had nineteen arches and stood for over six hundred years. There is an interesting model of it in the London Museum, which shows what a curiosity it was. Houses began to appear on it at an early date; in fact, the bridge was once one of the most fashionable places of residence in London. There was a tidying up in the eighteenth century, when many of the Nonsuch Palace style houses were rebuilt and the alcoves added. Several pieces of old London Bridge remain as memorials – an alcove in Victoria Park in the East End, a length of stone balustrade in Gilwell Park, Chingford, and there is another alcove at Guy's Hospital. These alcoves are always associated in my mind with the curious encounters of George Borrow with the apple woman in *Lavengro*, who owned a copy of *Moll Flanders*:

'A strange kind of bridge it was; huge and massive, and seemingly of great antiquity. It had an arched back like that of a hog, a high balustrade, and at either side, at intervals, were stone bowers bulking over the river, but open on the other side, and furnished with a semi-circular bench. Though the bridge was wide – very wide – it was all too narrow for the concourse upon it. Thousands of human beings were pouring over the bridge. . . . There I stood, just above the principal arch. . . . Towards the left bank of the river, a forest of masts, thick and close, as far as the eye could reach; spacious wharfs. . . . Before me, the troubled breast of the mighty river.'

Crowds still pour over the bridge, especially in the morning and evening rush, and the sounds of their tramping feet can be heard above the traffic. And they still stop to look over the balustrade, especially to the east, out over the Pool of London, for few can resist this, the finest river view in London – Billingsgate and the Custom House on the one side, wharves and warehouses from London Bridge to Tower Bridge on the other. Destitute men once slept under the landward arches of the Thames bridges. General Booth found 164 men taking shelter under Blackfriars

Bridge on a January night in 1870. At this period, the arches of London Bridge were also used for displaying posters.

Beer, bear gardens and Shakespeare are the thoughts one has on Bankside, still one of the most richly flavoured areas in London, wherein is the house I should wish to possess above any in London: the Cardinal's House, said to have been the residence of Wren during the building of St Paul's, a legend that can be taken with a grain of salt. In fact, Wren had several residences during this lengthy period, the one nearest to the Cathedral being across the river in Idol Lane.

I visit Southwark Cathedral at times for evensong and finish with a little private tour – looking at the ancient carved bosses, the tomb, now very highly coloured, of John Gower, the poet and friend of Chaucer, and other memorials, and musing on the possible grave of Edmund Shakespeare, the playwright's brother. He was buried here as were Philip Massinger and John Fletcher, but the positions of their graves are unknown. Shakespeare himself has a memorial in the Cathedral. He worked in Southwark from 1595 to 1611, at the two Bankside play-houses, the Swan and the Globe. One wonders what Shakespeare thought of the cruel bear baitings at Bankside, not that we can be complacent in view of the monstrous iniquity of vivisection. Long before then, the area had a queer reputation. It was a place of brothels in the Middle Ages, those who frequented them being rowed across the river from Stew Lane (stew meaning brothel).

The area from the foot of London Bridge westwards to the Power Station and along the Borough High Street as far as St George the Martyr Church has rich material and the charms of unexpected discovery for the London explorer. Ancient houses and courtyards are to be found next to industrial premises; in fact, this mixture is the keynote of the whole, notably in the juxtaposition of the Cathedral, railway arches and market. Examples of good cast iron work abound. The bollards of Clink Street, for example, are rare early specimens from the Napoleonic period – there is a pair of them outside the Anchor (drawing opposite). Mooney's at London Bridge has a decorative grill incorporating the words 'Mooneys Irish House' over the cellar door, and dotted round London Bridge Station are a few of the private lamp standards of the old South Eastern Railway Company, in the form of a bundle of spear handles bound by crossing bands, like the fasces of Imperial Rome.

Until fairly recently, a picturesque old house, very like the two still remaining at the time of writing in the Strand, stood in the Borough High Street. It was the premises of the Distil Coffee Company. When I went to look at it during the writing of this chapter, I found the place had vanished and a modern, no-style office block was on the site. Lant Street, too, where Bob Sawyer lodged, has been tidied up, and this process of erosion will be speeded up by the impending demolitions round London Bridge Station.

The formula for Bankside is to turn down one of the small, fruit-scented streets just before the Hop Exchange, threading away through the dark little Georgian streets – there is a concentration of them here – and out on to the river

Bankside
The Anchor

by the Anchor. The Anchor was condemned at one time, but the war saved it, and the new extension has been added without any loss of character to the old. The original Anchor – the one that stood in Shakespeare's time – was destroyed in the Southwark fire of 1676, and the present pub was built on the site of the old. It is the last of the famous taverns of Bankside. There are wonderful names here – Clink Street, Rose Alley, Globe Alley and Paris Gardens. The Anchor is a curious, rambling old pub, full of panelling, odd corners, concealed staircases and snuggeries. From the wharf in front, where a sort of platform has been built over the river for the greater enjoyment of the view, is one of the finest river panoramas in central London. It is part of the stretch of water known since the coronation of King George VI as 'The King's Reach'. St Paul's dome rises superbly above the blue grey warehouses of Broken Wharf Dock, Lyon's Wharf and Brooks's Wharf on the opposite bank. In the foreground, below the river wall, barges load and unload, but on Sunday a Sabbath peace and solitude reigns, profound enough to suit even the Lord's Day Observance Society.

Farther along Bankside, beside the Cardinal's House, there is a row of charming old houses with canopied doors, used as residences by members of the staff of Southwark Cathedral. Happy clerics! It is worth while taking on the thankless task of being about the Father's business in modern London in order to live in one of them. These old houses were left derelict for years after the war, and at one time seemed to be beyond hope of rescue; but the thing was done eventually.

Behind the Anchor is the Courage and Barclay Brewery, itself full of historical interest, apart from its associations with Dr Johnson. The commemorative plaque on the site of the Globe Theatre is in Park Street. It was provided by the Shakespeare Reading Society of London, and was originally erected in 1909 and unveiled by Sir H. Beerbohm Tree. The site is owned by Courage, Barclay and Simonds Limited and the plaque has been re-erected on the wall of the new bottling hall. No new archeological discoveries were made when this, the approximate site of the Globe, was excavated for the new building, but the brewery has a small museum containing a collection of relics, mostly pottery, that have been found on the site over a period of many years. The various fires and rebuildings since the Globe itself was destroyed by fire are sufficient to explain the paucity of the finds.

The Globe was erected in 1599, and fourteen years later in 1613 its thatched roof caught alight as a result of the firing of a cannon during a performance of *Henry VIII*. The building was destroyed in a couple of hours, one of the actors having his smouldering clothes put out by beer. A new Globe playhouse was erected in the following year, but it never achieved the success of its predecessor, and was demolished in 1644. The Brewery started in 1616, next to the Globe, and eventually covered the whole site. I had a fear that someone would build a replica of the Globe to mark the Shakespeare celebrations of 1964, a fear fortunately not realized. For my part, apron stages, audience participation and similar features of the Elizabethan stage are – at least in their present-day revival – wearisome in the extreme. I go to the theatre to enjoy myself, to be entertained, not to participate: I love illusion above all things, and am more than content to be separated from the business of the stage by the proscenium arch. It seems to me to be a mere archaism to dispense with the later refinements of the Renaissance in favour of more primitive arrangements: it is certain that the present-day advocates of apron stages and similar contrivances would stop short at a revival of Elizabethan playhouse manners – the eating, the talk, the drinking of beer and cracking of nuts. . . .

Perhaps the most interesting relic here is the large section of wall, and part of the great rose window of the extensive Winchester Palace, the home of the Bishops of Winchester from 1106 to 1649, in Clink Street. Wolsey lived here, and Henry VIII was entertained at the Palace. It survived in a ruinous state until the fire of 1814. After that, nineteenth-century warehouses were built into it, covering up the ancient stonework until work began on the new fruit warehouse of Messrs J. O. Sims. The wall, part of which is in my drawing, rises up through three stories, ending in the rose window at present being uncovered by the Ministry of Works on what is now the roof of the new building. Down below, you can see the old buttresses and other ancient stonework that was here in place when Shakespeare walked past on his way to the Globe.

As recently as three years ago, when my *City Sights* was published, Upper and Lower Thames Street were all but intact, apart from sites cleared by wartime bombing. Its architecture – wharf and warehouses, church and alley and what-not – was admittedly a conglomeration, but of work of good periods. Now this casual, agreeable pattern is being rapidly broken up, and the result is considerably less satisfactory. The prospect under the arch of London Bridge is now terminated by the monstrous block opposite the Custom House, entirely out of harmony with its surroundings. The new extension to the Custom House is an exception, being an admirable exercise in the style of the early nineteenth century; nothing else would have done.

Nevertheless, this walk from Blackfriars to the Tower remains one of my favourite London perambulations. At one time, one could count on enjoying it in a solitude unbroken, apart from a distant prospect of an occasional policeman or someone drawing in one of the narrow, ancient lanes leading down to the river, with perhaps a City cat, employed at a warehouse, taking a leisurely stroll. Here again is change. Visitors to the Tower make their way along here – Americans, Frenchmen, those from what we hopefully call 'the Commonwealth' and contingents from all over Britain. Most are armed with cameras. Some listen to transistors as they walk along. The man in the Monument sits on his chair outside and watches this stream of sightseers, as (most of them having knocked themselves up by climbing to the top of the column) they fade off to Tower Hill.

You can begin the tour from Blackfriars, where there is a number of curious, old lanes immediately to the right of Ludgate Hill: Carter Lane, with its old dairy, the Apothecaries Hall, well worth taking in your stride, the old churchyard, grim and desolate, of St Anne, Blackfriars, together with Wardrobe Place, where any of Dickens's impecunious solicitors' clerks or their employers might have lived, and Playhouse Yard. As my drawing shows, Playhouse Yard is of antique appearance, at least on one side, though none of the remaining buildings, in spite of their age, appears to have any connexion with the theatres which stood here in the reign of Queen Elizabeth I. They had a complicated history which has been the subject of patient investigation, but for general purpose all that need be said is that the players were quartered in the remains of the Blackfriars Monastery, established for the Dominicans by Hubert de Burgh, Earl of Kent, in 1221. Shakespeare's company played Blackfriars during the winter where their patrons were rather more select than those of Bankside.

The names of the ancient alleys never fail to intrigue me as I walk along – Stew Lane, Coffee House Alley, Trig Lane and the rest. Many of them have steps leading down to the river, and it requires little effort of imagination to dream up a vision of the richness of the place in the time of Elizabeth, with the boats coming in to Queenhithe and Puddle Dock, the Swan Uppings (marking of the cygnets with the device of the owners – mainly the Crown and the Dyers' and Vintners' Companies – on the upper mandible), and the rich pageants.

66

Apostles- Cannon Street

The wealthy London Fishmongers, of whom Sir William Walworth, who saved the life of Richard II, was the most famous, were buried in the churches of the area, as indeed was Dick Whittington. Many of the Thames-side churches were not reconstructed after the Fire. Even so, the number rebuilt by Wren in this small area was considerable. The churchyard of All Hallows is today a mass of weeds and debris, broken walls and rubbish; nothing could be more melancholy. By its side rise the twin towers of Cannon Street Station (drawing opposite) and great flanking wall, all that now remains of this vast Victorian terminus. These cupolas are in the best tradition of nineteenth-century engineering architecture; they add something to the City skyline, as seen from as far away as Waterloo Bridge. There is some hope that they will be preserved in the rebuilding. Cannon Street was built by the old South Eastern Railway between 1864 and 1866, and designed by John Hawkshaw and E. M. Barry; the front – the old Cannon Street Hotel – was similar to Barry's still existing Charing Cross Hotel, in a style that only the Victorians could have achieved. A restless mongrel Belgian Renaissance is the nearest approximation one can think of.

Another forgotten Thames Street churchyard, now partly built over by the new Salvation Army International Headquarters building, is that of St Peter's, Paul's Wharf, a church destroyed in the Great Fire. I went to look at the pathetic remains of it while making the drawings for this book; no one would ever dream today that there was a garden here once, with laburnums and lilacs. The dead have been carted away: they were just a nuisance. All I found among the rubbish were a few struggling spikes of willowherb, from which the silky sugar stealers were taking off to colonize elsewhere. There were piles of old, rotting newspapers, wet rags and old tin cans, and I surprised a pigeon who was having forty winks between clumps of weeds and an old boot.

Old brick warehouses lean over Trig Lane. At its far end, a gas lamp burns, a chrome yellow flame behind its cracked glass. I made the drawing at the end of this chapter towards sunset on a Sunday in winter. Shapeless, grey clouds fumbled their way across a dun coloured sky that was enlivened only by a streak of orange to the west, over Blackfriars Bridge. There was hardly any sound at all, apart from the occasional rumble of the railway, the cry of a seagull and the lapping water. Swans were resting in a little pool formed by a bar of gravel and the huge posts, yellow green with slime, were reflected in the river. I poked about on the beach to study its geology, and found it to be made up of bottles, flints, fragments of brick made smooth by tides, bits of pottery, glass and oyster shells, all embedded in mud and sand. There was a strange red moss in the pools left in the mud banks. Its slowly waving filaments were the colour of blood; from a few yards distance, the effect was similar to the muddy, blood-tinted puddles one used to see in the gutters outside slaughter houses in the bad old days.

Queenhithe, the subject of my other Thames Street drawing (on the next page), was once the principal dock of London. It dates from the reign of Alfred, but it

acquired its present name in the reign of Henry II. Fish were once landed here, as at Billingsgate. Today it is only an inlet in the line of warehouses, but the open square behind Thames Street gives an idea of its original size. Here are monumental warehouses of blackened stone and brick, fit subjects for Meryon to etch. The colour of the dock is a study in black and greys, for mud is silver grey at low tide, and the only note of colour is the red paint on the barges. Queenhithe is almost certainly the harbour or anchorage of Roman London.

VI

The Fun of Battersea Park

———— * ————

THERE are times when the central Thames is singularly beautiful. On a sunlit autumn afternoon, especially, the home-going crowds across Waterloo Bridge are treated to a sight of Turneresque or Impressionist brilliance. Tints of golden green on the Embankment trees turn to the colour of copper beeches, almost as the setting sun tinges the London sky with red. The harsh features of Victorian and modern blocks are softened into flat planes of blue-grey, mauve-grey and in the distance an ineffable golden grey, which is the Houses of Parliament. The sunlight is reflected back in a dazzling path on the river, and soft blue shadows lurk in the carvings of Cleopatra's Needle. Once, before the trams went, the scene was even more satisfying as the light faded and trams made golden and red blurs behind the plane trees. But it is still good, in spite of the absence of trams. St Martin's spire catches the dying light of the autumn day, and birds wheel around Nelson. Turn away to the City, and all the riverside is veiled in the filmy blue mist peculiar to London; a few golden lights, now on the Discovery's masts, now on the dome of St Paul's or far away on ships sliding down the river, bring out the poetry and mystery of the Thames.

Once, too, this whole stretch bordering the Strand was full of mansions and great houses – Leicester House, later Essex House, Somerset House, the Palace of John of Gaunt. This, of 'time honoured Lancaster', finished up ignominiously enough: what remained of it was acquired by the directors of the Royal Cobourg Theatre (now the Old Vic) when the present building was going up in the early nineteenth century. Stone from the Strand Palace of John of Gaunt was used for the foundations sunk into that waterlogged ground of Lower Marsh.

Essex House stood in the Strand, opposite St Clement Danes. What we think of as a comparatively recent innovation – the demolition of old houses and subsequent rebuilding at a higher density on their sites – began at least as far back as 1675, when Nicholas Barbon, London's first real speculative builder, bought Essex House, pulled it down and built Essex Street on the site. Several fine old houses, some with panelling and staircases with twisted 'barley sugar' balustrades still remain. At the end is the Water Gate, damaged during the war, and restored. This was built to ensure seclusion from the commercial wharves Barbon was building on the river. Essex House was used for legal business during the Great Fire, and Pepys was present there in January 1669, at a meeting of naval officers. He describes the place as 'large but ugly'.

Devereux Court runs off Essex Street to the gateway, which leads into Fountain Court, and then turns north into Fleet Street. It has two pubs of interest. The Essex Head, where Dr Johnson established an evening club in 1783, is at the corner of Essex Street. 'The terms', the doctor wrote in a letter, 'are lax and the expenses light. We meet thrice a week, and he who misses forfeits twopence.' The present pub is Victorian, recently refurbished, but some of the decorative late nineteenth-century engraved, gilded and embossed mirror glass fortunately remains. At the far end of the Court is The Devereux with a bust of the Earl of Essex, who was one of the leading Parliamentary generals in the Civil War. It was once the famous Grecian Coffee House. Before being turned into a tavern, it was the meeting place of Addison, Steele, Goldsmith, Sir Isaac Newton and other men of literature and scholarship.

It is a great pity that the extension to King's College will not only sweep away the two ancient houses which give so much character to the Strand but also the old Watch House in Strand Lane (drawing over the page). Strand Lane runs down to the Victoria Embankment from St Mary le Strand. The house, Regency at the back, has a pretty cast-iron canopied balcony looking down towards the river and overlooking the Roman Bath where David Copperfield had a cold plunge. Although all this will be built over, the bath is to be preserved – it may perhaps have a use for the cooling of undergraduates' heads – but all the delightful charm Londoners can now enjoy will disappear for good.

Strand Lane is very little used. The exit at the river end is now blocked up, but readers of Dickens will remember that Mr Percy Noakes, law student of Gray's Inn and a devilish good fellow, was conveyed from there to the *Endeavour*, off the Custom House, as manager of a certain water party that ended in disaster. Occasionally one sees a solitary wanderer, obviously off course, or a pair of King's College students talking together. They all turn up the Surrey Steps, under the Norfolk Hotel, half-way down. Green, worn and old are the flagstones of Strand Lane, and several fine old pillar gas lamps remain, with another on the wall of the passage-way by the side of the Watch House.

Three cast iron boundary marks are worth noting here – one at the far end of the Lane and two others by the Watch House, marking the bounds of the parishes of St Mary le Strand and St Clement Danes. The care with which London parishes were parcelled out is illustrated by two of these marks, both belonging to St Mary le Strand; that by the Embankment has the measurement 4 *ft.* 3 *in. East*, the other, on the wall of the passage way, 7 *ft.* 8½ *in. East*.

At the corner of Surrey Street and Howard Street is the Victorian perpendicular Gothic pub, the Cheshire Cheese, with rather splendid iron railings to the area and an oriel window. Next door, is another pub the Edwardian Surrey, where Australian beer is supplied on draught. At the very top of the street is the Australian gift shop (I love gift shops even more than birth control shops) where you can buy toy Koala bears and tins of Kangaroo soup.

Other dark entries still exist at Charing Cross – one, in particular, to the west of the station, dark, Doré-ish and damp, lit by an uneasy gas lamp and cobbled. There is the oddly named 'Of Alley', with a morbid, unattractive lavatory in the middle, smelling like a salmon tin. The streets round here were named after George Villiers, Duke of Buckingham – George Street, Villiers Street and so forth. 'Of' was all that was left for the alley. The Arches are on my regular visiting list, for here many of the choice half-wits, deadbeats and vagabonds of London gravitate, sometimes with guitars, all strongly in contrast with its war-time history, when it filled up each night with Londoners armed with thermos flasks, blankets and individual fruit pies.

The bridges at this part of the river, Hungerford, have at least one thing to recommend them – the magnificent views they offer of the Houses of Parliament.

The mention of half-wits reminds me of a recent curious incident which occurred to me lower down the river at Lambeth. I had been drawing the Archbishop's garden (where incidentally are some of the finest Trees of Heaven in London – a tree which, like the plane, withstands the London atmosphere), had admired the Tudor gateway, one of the few left in London, and wandered as dusk fell into Lambeth Parish Church. I was absorbed in the details of the building, and only came to the surface when the door closed to with a noise fit to waken up Captain Bligh in the churchyard; I found myself locked in. It never occurred to me to toll the bell. What I did was to scramble up to a window ledge, hoping to attract the attention of people going home across the path. I found to my dismay that the few who came below the window were scared stiff (this is absolutely true) and sheered off, evidently under the impression I was a visitor from the next world. They shook their heads and passed by on the other side in inconceivable stupidity. At length, as I grew weary, someone stopped (by now only a few minutes remained before dark and the church was already pitch black inside); he brought a sensible London bobby, who ultimately brought the Rector to my rescue.

From here it is an easy expedition to Vauxhall. Not a trace of its former glories – tawdry, perhaps, by daylight – remain. It was the first of the big London riverside pleasure gardens, followed by Ranelagh, on the site where the Chelsea Flower Show is now held, Cremorne, of which only a gateway remains, its grounds being at first turned into allotments ('Lots') and then being covered by the Power Station, and finally Battersea, recent and not fully disinfected from Socialist jollity. Vauxhall was a pleasure ground as early as the seventeenth century, when it was known as the Spring Gardens, but its great period began about 1728 and continued until the 1840s.

There were groves of trees filled with lamps, colonnades of supper-boxes, a Chinese Temple, cascades, fireworks and balloon ascents.

Strand Lane

Oh! the balloon, the great balloon
It left Vauxhall one Monday at noon.

You can read about it, if you wish, in the *Ingoldsby Legends* and get a contemporary account of the gardens in the Sketches by Boz.

Now, if you go down Vauxhall way, looking for the site (a little way inland from Vauxhall Bridge) of that vanished pleasaunce, you will not find daffodils that have come from Chelsea nor violets down from Kew, but only waste paper blown about by the riverside winds, dust and thundering lorries from Nine Elms. One fragment of eighteenth-century Vauxhall remains. This is Brunswick House, with a semi-circular porch ornamented with swags and rams' heads, in the Adam style. Wharves prevent access to the river for most of the way, and the landscape is grim and industrialized. You go over the railway bridge to the Battersea Dogs' Home, where two charming statues of dogs beg from the gate. When I was writing the notes for this chapter, I thought I ought to go in and look round but, having experienced the heartbreak of dogs' homes in the past, I funked it and left a donation instead. The place is marvellously run, but a fearful temptation to those like myself who cannot resist dogs.

Battersea Park, landscaped out of earth taken from the dock excavations of the Isle of Dogs, is a great consolation for South Londoners. On my last visit the deer were temporarily out of residence, their places being taken by a flock of black sheep which contentedly cropped the grassy mound. That sheep may safely graze, ring doves coo in shady elms and ducks splash the sunny afternoons away within a few minutes of the horrors of Nine Elms is just one of the violent contrasts of London. The boating lake, sparkling in the sun, is an invitation to escape, at least temporarily, from the close confinement of the Battersea streets; so is the children's zoo, perhaps one of the most agreeable parts of the Fun Fair. After long residence, the Indian mynah birds have acquired a wonderful repertoire of wolf whistles, which they practise on teenage girls with hideous realism.

The visitors add a touch of music hall humour. A woman says 'Hullo, darling,' to the toucan, 'you've come off the Guinness poster', thereby proving beyond all doubt the force of advertising. You see fat women and small boys' uncles teasing the chimpanzee, and wonder at the terrible resemblance: what troubles the mind is not the likeness of the humans to the monkey tribe, but the likeness of the humans to yourself – that is the fearful thing. There was a goat and her kid contemplating these things when I was there last, and a donkey also lost in thought, pensively staring out at the visitors from his pen, an inscrutable expression on his features. The fact is these animals know us to be fools, but are obliged to cover up their disgust. One fat lady there had given the chimp a yo-yo. She had one herself, and they were both yo-yoing together – he on the inside of the bars and his benefactor outside. It was a sight too profound for anyone but Darwin.

I sought to cheer myself up by touring the fun fair and commenced by buying a ballpoint pen with the figures of two cuties on it: their undergarments slip off as you use the pen. Thus encouraged, I toured the penny in the slot machines, and made this drawing. There are machines all over the fair; over it all drifts the smell of hamburgers, against a musical background of 'Mexicale Rose', 'Carolina Moon' and up-to-date pop records of hideous cacophony. I love the 'Knock the Lady in the Water' show ('Knock the lady in the water, guv'nor. Seven balls a shillin' '). The outfit consists of a brunette in bed, surrounded by draped net curtains and artificial flowers in a chromium stand – a vertitable boudoir, you think, though perhaps a trifle too breezy for complete comfort. Old men and chewing youths goggle – no doubt struck dumb by the curious way the brunette has chosen to earn her living.

The Love Test machine is one of the few ancient ones, built originally, I should guess, before the Great War and subsequently modernized. It has a thermometer of sorts in

which the liquid hovers and finally settles. I tried it, but could only get it up as far as 'Warm, you should get off easily', which, in view of the other possibilities, was very tame.

I tried the fortune-telling gypsy, who nods her head epileptically and delivers a card, all for a penny. She was more encouraging, and pointed out that 'although financial matters have been the cause of some recent worry, these will be a thing of the past before you are much older'. I studied my fortune while waiting for the boat to start on the world cruise. 'The Coolest Ride in the Park'. It was like the River Caves I patronized so

extensively at Blackpool when I was a small boy (when I noticed the floating Woodbine and Star cigarette packets, I knew I was growing up).

'Yo can't go round de world yet, mister,' said a cheerful West Indian girl. 'De boats won't go until Chris comes back.' So I waited the return of the wonder-working Chris, who at length came and sent me on my way to Canada, Malta, Holland, gliding past Egypt, where I noticed the Sphinx had a queer cast in its eye, India represented by the Taj Mahal, and Rome, where a model of St Peter's represented all the rest like a Member of Parliament. We also visited Windsor Castle, where the water was full of Krunchy-Snax bags, floating on the tide, a thing Queen Victoria would never have allowed for an instant.

When you have recovered your land legs, you can visit the Grotto. Nothing is more to my taste, especially a cockney Grotto. The weather had changed while I was on my world cruise, naturally, and the thunder rumbled violently as I made the drawing on the previous page, giving me extra value for my sixpence. I was promised the cave of the winds, the cave of the volcano and the cave of the water, but a thunderstorm turned the whole enterprise into a decided bargain, as well as increasing the realism, for the thunder made the grotto shake. It is one of the best sixpennyworths in London, and has suitably matured since I first visited it when the gardens were being laid out; virginia creeper now hangs luxuriantly over the entrance. The water cave is distinctly impressive. Lights change on a fountain which rises to the roof and falls, splashing heavily into the pool below. The charmed spectator descends the cave down a flight of steps, and you can gaze down into the pool and think of the joy of having a private grotto (I had the place to myself for a long time) like Pope's, also on the river, at Twickenham. As I meditated, watching the rise and fall of the waters, a man in overalls appeared below in the dark. Did the good lady who keeps the grotto (another joy – putting on income tax returns, 'Trade or Profession – Grotto Keeper') think I was out-staying my welcome? At last, I departed, by the cave with the luminous plants to the final cave where a waterfall drops into a pool. The rain still came down, and the thunder rolled from a green and purple sky. The man in overalls was sweeping away the water at the door, like Dame Partington. 'I shouldn't go out this way, if I were you,' he remarked to me, 'the water's coming into the bloody grotto.'

VII

Chelsea Moods

———— * ————

CHELSEA BRIDGE is ugly, but from it are fine views of sky, water, trees and the Albert Bridge (above), a cobwebby, fairy-like structure, Victorian ironwork at its best. It was designed by R. W. Ordish and built in 1873. On the day just described, the sky had turned to green and gold, and was heavy with indigo clouds. I turned back to look at Battersea Power Station, and was struck with its dramatic effect; the main part of the building was in shadow and dull red, only the chimney stacks and the slowly curling plumes of smoke from them caught the sunlight; in the foreground the bridge was a lattice of dark grey, all against the thunder clouds. The mutations of the English climate give an astonishing range of effects over the Thames; one can never have enough of them.

79

Opposite the Barracks, as I have said, is the site of Ranelagh, always more aristocratic than Vauxhall. Its most important feature was the Rotunda, built in 1741. Canaletto's painting of its interior is in the National Gallery and shows a throng of beaux and belles parading the area around the great central pier, which was also a fireplace, under the chandeliers. It was a place for masques, fancy balls, promenading and assignments. Mozart appeared there, and Handel also, playing his own compositions on a small chamber organ, including such pieces as the *Dixit Dominus*, Handel's choral setting of Psalm 110, for the musical entertainments were by no means always light in character.

I have much fondness for the Chelsea Flower Show and its vast marquee, full of keen gardeners, rural deans, sturdy women and oversized exhibits. I love to amble past the stands of the horticultural firms, eyeing the shimmering greenhouses, lawn mowers, bird baths and plastic gnomes, listening to the band playing under the chestnuts – selections from Ivor Novello or else the overture, 'The Bronze Horse'. On Chelsea Show days I always follow the same ritual, and come out with the crowd to Lyons Teashop in Sloane Square where, for four days in the year, the accents are anything but metropolitan and those of the North strongly represented. The Yorkists and Lancastrians need no rose badge to distinguish them; even if you were deaf, you could identify them at once by their new, uncomfortable suits and their good humour, not to mention the loads of food laced with truly astonishing quantities of brown sauce and tomato ketchup they manage to pack away.

Paradise itself apart, there are only three places in which to live the good life in perfection – Albany, Hampstead and Chelsea; it hardly matters which. When I lived in Chelsea, I used to love to shop for and cook my own food, and a girl who was one of the considerable offspring of a notable artist (at least she called him 'Daddy') used to come and eat up my slender rations. When I was in funds, I dined at the Blue Cockatoo which, in those days, was still owned by the proprietor who started it in 1914. There is a marvellous view of the river and the delightful Albert Bridge from the windows. The atmosphere was very strongly charged with a 1910–1914 feeling, which one could easily intensify by thinking of the pre-Great War Slade and reading old copies of the *Studio* and *Connoisseur*. This period quality is not easily conveyed in prose for it is much too volatile, but it can be caught from the intimate interiors of Orpen, Tonks and Steer, some of John's sketches and, in fact, most of the Slade productions of that golden age. Two paintings especially give off this subtle bouquet – a river scene of 1914, a mother and child and big umbrella, in the Manchester Art Gallery by Philip Connard and the same artist's 'Chelsea Interior' in the Oldham Art Gallery, in which the Slade-Chelsea atmosphere of the years before the Great War is delightfully preserved. In both, and in many of these paintings, the undertones of sadness, below the apparent tranquillity, can be felt by anyone moderately sensitive.

Another of my favourite Chelsea moods is more easily indulged in – the Oscar

Wilde mood in Tite Street. Some of the late Victorian studios and flats have had their brickwork cleaned, including Oscar's house, now numbered 34 (the veritable Castle Bunbury) and the house adjoining. Otherwise the bricks of the houses in this part of the street have mostly dirtied to a dingy grey brown. In spite of the hideous new lamps, it is possible to slip into the period mood without much difficulty, and I have often stood on the steps and imagined letting myself in after an orgy with young men or after sending my guests home delighted with the food, wine, and, best of all, the conversation I have offered them at the Café Royal or simply standing there giving Queensberry a dose of searing wit. Then I go inside, take off my fur coat and lavender kid gloves, and gloat over my drawings by Aubrey Beardsley.

Most of the houses on this side are intact, as Wilde and Whistler knew them, and have interesting late Victorian ironwork to their areas, in that curious bastard classical of the 1880s. This style, although with elements of Norman Shaw in its composition, has been given no label; for convenience, I call it 'early Wilde'. Wilde's house is divided into flats, and a line of clothes pegs or washing is to be seen sometimes in the balcony of the attic window, an arrangement which would have laid Lady Bracknell out for the entire London season. The street door is the original, and you think of Robert Ross slipping through it to gather up a few of Wilde's treasures for his friend before the hideous sale.

Lower down is the vast Tower House, staring red, 1885, with its huge studio window (those were the *great* days) and cut brick cornices, with the inevitable sunflower and marigolds carved in the metopes. Another faded relic of the heyday of the Victorian R.A. and the picture of the year is More Lodge, now gloomy, dirty, all but deserted. A bust of More is over the door of the porch. The glass in the narrow windows is damaged and obscured with dust. But it has at least survived, being luckier in that respect than Whistler's White House, which I drew for this book (next page) as a record shortly before its demolition. Harry Quilter, who acquired the place after Whistler's bankruptcy, and one or two later occupiers modified the house as left by Whistler, but enough remained to enable one to appreciate its qualities and imagine the sensation its severity occasioned in late Victorian Chelsea. It was a marvellous Chelsea, this of Whistler, Wilde, Carlyle, Swinburne. Sometimes I get myself addled with imagining it – those wonderful days when Rossetti was painting dreamy, languorous, long-necked women at the house in Cheyne Walk, when the river, before the Embankments and the granite walls came in 1870–4, lapped peacefully, in beauty, on its sandy beach, when Whistler was rowed on the river by the Greaves brothers and the female Blondin performed at Cremorne!

Round the corner and a short distance along Cheyne Walk is Norman Shaw at his most picturesque and agreeable. This is Swan House, no. 17. The metal doors have swans in the upper panels and a kind of honeysuckle ornament in the lower, but the chief charm of the design belongs to the three large bay windows, divided

81

into small leaded panes and overhanging panels of garlands, fruit and strapwork, with a swan in the centre. It is possible to forgive him New Scotland Yard and the Piccadilly Hotel when admiring this delightful façade behind the plane trees.

Then come the fine houses of the eighteenth century, including Rossetti's – shady gardens, cast-iron work, all delightful. Old Chelsea figures in the shape of old age pensioners sit in the Embankment gardens, by Ford Madox Brown's memorial to Rossetti, and feed the birds, though the wonder is that the deafening, non-stop traffic along the Embankment has not driven them out of the district long ago.

Near to Chelsea church is Turner's cottage, where he gazed on his last sunset, saying 'The Sun is God' before sinking on his pillow in death. Chelsea church is a miracle of restoration, owing its existence to the love the Rector and parishioners had for it. The capitals in the More chapel, said to be by Holbein and certainly rich and unusual, mercifully escaped the bombing. The interior with its ancient monuments is full of interest and peace and feeling of ancient days. There are chained books – the only ones now remaining in any London church – given by Sir Hans Sloane, and the box-like classic nave opens into the medieval chancel and chapels, all superbly put together again after the war. The exterior, too, is

quaint in the right sense – I mean, full of character – where the vine grows over the monument to Sir Hans Sloane and lilies and hollyhocks bloom in the garden.

It is a true village church of the old Chelsea – the Chelsea still to be seen in Church Street, Justice Walk and Cheyne Row, though increasingly threatened by the traffic men, the Government bureaucrats who wish to use Chelsea as a dump for hospitals and other choice institutions and private developers. None of these has evidently the slightest feeling for the area or those who live in it. Fulham, Putney and Hammersmith (apart from the houses on or near the Mall) have been debauched long ago – only Chelsea retains its atmosphere and that village character delightfully recorded by Walter Greaves in etchings, drawings and paintings; he loved Chelsea, no one more so. His painting of 'Chelsea Regatta' in the Manchester Art Gallery brings back vividly the village life in Chelsea in the middle of the last century, though it is not so well known, nor so decorative, as his delightful 'Hammersmith Bridge on Boat Race Day' at the Tate.

He went on painting pictures of Chelsea until he was an old man, when he used to say, 'Old Battersea Bridge (the curious old wooden one replaced by the present dull affair built by Bazalgette in 1886–90) got a bit on the minds of us all.' Greaves's painting of Hammersmith shows the suspension bridge of 1827, which somewhat resembled Marlow Suspension Bridge. The present one, even more charming, is another of Bazalgette's designs and dates from 1884–7. What with his bridges (Putney drawn on page 91 is another), his Embankment and sewerage schemes, his pumping stations and the Woolwich Ferry, Bazalgette did a lot to the Thames, usually well on the credit side.

Church Street is especially agreeable, and small modern houses have been admirably fitted in to a collection mainly Georgian. I never omit to look at the old dairy, where cows were kept up to 1914. It is now a patisserie. Two tiled panels of the Walter Crane – George Mason school of the 1880s remain – a countryman, idealized, of course, and a dairymaid straight out of 'Patience'. Near the cornice is a cow's head in gold. The shippon remains in the mews and there are nice bits of engraved glass in the shop.

Along the river is another Chelsea curiosity – the medieval Crosby·Hall, transferred from Bishopsgate where it was originally the dining hall of Sir John Crosby's house, ending its days there as a restaurant. It was taken to bits and rebuilt at Chelsea in 1910. It is still being used for dining, being now part of the International Hall of Residence of the British Federation of University Women and is at present being extended so that food can be supplied from under the gallery – the usual position for serving food in a medieval hall. The blank end as seen in my drawing on the next page is where the work stopped in 1910.

The stretch of river known as Chelsea Reach is still very Whistlerian at dusk; the dull warehouses and factories on the Battersea shore have not forgotten what Whistler did for them and continually come up with effects similar to his 'Old Battersea Bridge' – the Nocturne in Blue and Gold in the Tate Gallery. Down the

reach is the Albert Bridge (not a true suspension bridge, actually). Its clustered columns, attached to four pinnacled piers, and delicate ironwork make it the most decorative bridge in London. It cannot be admired too often. Everything about it is right, including the wooden toll-houses and well-designed gas lamps. Nothing in Chelsea is more delightful than a view of it in winter, through a foreground of bare branches, from the window of the Blue Cockatoo or from the side of the Embankment, almost head on; the structure curves dramatically towards the spectator. The great arch in the foreground and the iron bracing are violently foreshortened; on the Battersea side the other arch is blue grey, although only the river's width away. It is a Whistlerian harmony in blue and grey, with rich olive in the shadow of the piers, and passing oil tankers giving sharper notes of black and crimson. As night comes on, the lights of Battersea fun fair and park, strung out along the trees, give a touch of Oriental fantasy; one thinks of Hong Kong or Shanghai.

Near the Blue Cockatoo and the Pier Hotel is the yard leading to the old forge and the billiard table works. I wandered up there when Thurston's had just removed, and I meditated on a pile of old and dusty mahogany billiard table legs, heavy and elaborately turned, that mouldered under a shed. Billiard tables still remain stubbornly nineteenth century, and are possibly the only Victorian furniture still in production. At any rate, they are worth the connoisseur's attention, and I value them along with bentwood chairs, dressmaker's dummies, hatstands, chlorodyne, gripewater, Fennings Fever Mixture and Salvation Army bonnets as life-giving survivals of the golden age.

Beyond Battersea Bridge are the floating Bohemians and their wives, the only Chelsea women to walk the plank. The colony is housed in a collection of multi-coloured craft of various sorts, mostly of wartime vintage, with a few old Thames barges. I have on one or two occasions been on the point of acquiring one of the best ones (some seem in an advanced state of decay) to use as a floating studio; but the noise of traffic along the Embankment is now considerable, and one must be very thoroughly Bohemian to stomach the lines of washing, close proximity to one's fellows and the roof-top dustbins. Moreover, although the Thames is becoming cleaner (a shoal of porpoises were seen in the Thames at Dagenham in 1965), the river is still far from pleasant whenever the weather is hot. A friend of mine, a confirmed Chelseaite, described them to me as 'floating pig stys' – a somewhat harsh generalization, to which there are notable exceptions. Nonetheless, the general impression is not entirely prepossessing (drawing on pages 88–89). Various busybodies have stirred themselves from time to time to introduce schemes for forcible tidying up of these floating palaces. In that they will be successful, sooner or later, for Bohemianism is ever only skin deep in bourgeois England. There is nothing we hate more than a refusal to conform, and nothing we approve more than a meddlesome busybody.

Swans preen themselves at low tide, haughtily ignoring the kids who play about in the mud and driftwood. Opposite is Wilson Steer's home for many years, no. 108 Cheyne Walk, where Tonks and George Moore and other old men used to come for cosy evenings and where Steer (not unmindful perhaps of Whistler's portrait of his mother) painted his fine and affectionate portrait of his housekeeper, Mrs. Raynes. A lot of rubbish was written at the time of his death about Steer's landscapes and his love of beach subjects at low tide. In fact (and I have it on the authority of a friend of his who frequently accompanied him on his summer travels), Steer chose them mostly because of their proximity to a lavatory, as artists often, or should, do.

This brings me to a favourite Chelsea subject, the cast-iron lavatory at the end of Cheyne Walk, (drawing at the end of this chapter), one of the best of a vanishing race. It is one of the kind one would love to possess and go mad over and have erected in one's back yard or garden. This Chelsea specimen is the only one I know that is fitted with gargoyles. The front is divided into six panels – delicate, late Victorian ornament below an upright grille, then a sort of Elizabethan strap-work pattern; the panels with the Victorian ornament have the pattern composed of small holes for ventilation. The maker's name appears in a circular device also on the front: 'SARACEN FOUNDRY, GLASGOW. Macfarlane's Patent'. Wonderful to own a foundry where lavatories are cast, and then to give it so bloodthirsty a name! As for Macfarlane, he was a benefactor to the race, and his name ought to be cherished along with the rest of those eminent Victorians who invented and patented a variety of other conveniences to solace us in our earthly pilgrimage – Mr Rowland with his Macassar oil, Beecham and Holloway with their pills and, last but not least, Mr Simpson of more recent years who delighted my school days with his iodine lockets.

Lots Road Power Station was built in 1914 on the site, as I have said, of Cremorne Gardens. It is now being modernized, but I hope the rebuilding will spare the tree, the last survivor of that Arcadian place, which still grows in a corner of the yard. The Balloon Tavern and one of the entrance gates of Cremorne are other reminders of vanished Cockney delights in a barren waste of crumbling brick – Stadium Street, Burnaby Road – the Chelsea nobody wants, full of coloured kids roller-skating among grim little decaying terraces with gothicky bay windows and depressing railings. Soon the World's End district will be redeveloped, and the dreary houses where many of the Slade models lived will be replaced by a self-contained village of flats, shopping centre, school, church and other dreary contrivances, all, without doubt, just as depressing as the district is now.

There is a good view of the fine eighteenth-century church of Battersea where William Blake was married (Turner also visited it to sketch from the vestry window) from the Chelsea Basin, with the new flats towering behind the spire and dwarfing it and another, with industrial foreground, from the power station wharf.

I wish I could devote more space to Chelsea, where there is always something special and lively in the air. All I have done is merely to select a few from a long

list of possibilities. There are the pubs and restaurants, the slums, all charming to me, St Luke's church, Chelsea Palace (soon, I hope, to return to variety), where once I saw Jack the Giant Killer stuck fast on his own beanstalk, the quiet squares pre-eminently civilized, the delights of the King's Road, the curious atmosphere of Carlyle's house, the Botanic Garden. We would have needed no passport to Pimlico, and, had time allowed, could have visited St Barnabas, an interesting Gothic Revival church with unusual features, and gazed with admiration in the windows of the second-hand clothes shop, with the top boots for sale, and old-fashioned haberdashers where they still sell flowery aprons and cards of buttons.

We have hardly glanced at Sloane Square, the only Continental square in London. These ought not to be lightly dismissed. As it is, we must press on up river to Putney, taking the towpath in the direction of Hammersmith.

Cast iron
Riverside Lavatory, Chelsea

Putney Bridge

VIII

The Pubs of Hammersmith

━━━━━━ ✳ ━━━━━━

PUTNEY, of course, means the Boat Race, one of the few genuinely amateur sporting events yet remaining and still a private affair between Oxford and Cambridge. Walter Greaves's painting of the old Hammersmith Bridge shows what Boat Race crowds were like in the Victorian age; in those days the towpath between Putney and Mortlake was packed with sightseers, religious cranks and hawkers, forming a sort of Thames-side Derby Day, with a similar carnival atmosphere.

St Mary's, the Parish Church of Putney, is now completely dwarfed by a great slab-like office block, as my drawing shows, and the two blocks on the opposite

91

from Putney Pier
58 [signature]

side do nothing to improve the riverside of Fulham. It is better to turn one's back to this, and appreciate the Star and Garter Hotel. Its style – mongrel French Renaissance combined with a suggestion of music-hall architecture carried out in red brick and white stone – gives one a feeling of being on one of the quays by the Seine, an idea reinforced by the cyclists, trees and parked cars. For a moment, a Parisian would feel perfectly at home. Colonies of swans favour the Putney riverside, along with the ducks. Sparrows and pigeons also compete for bread and scraps, and tempers here among the feathery tribe are inclined to be sharp in the cold weather.

Besides the pub and the wild life of the river, there are two other enjoyments at the foot of Putney Bridge – the lavatory possessing a mosaic floor in browns and black, good enough for a Roman villa, and the second-hand furniture emporium opposite, with its cast-iron front and door guarded by the figures of two cherubic infants.

The best of Putney is, however, the view from the pier (above), looking towards Hammersmith. My drawing was made on a day of rapidly moving cloud and brilliant spring sunshine which sparkled on the river. There were sudden spurts of rain and brilliant distant lights on trees far away. Flags, boathouses and poplars combined with the expanses of sky and green water, rippling in bright pale blue and catching dissolving points of cream colour from the clouds, to make a Sisley or a Dufy – all looseness and light.

From Putney to Hammersmith by the riverside is one of the most agreeable walks in London, and on many afternoons you can enjoy it in almost uninterrupted solitude – not too lonely for comfort, that is, for you can have the swans for company, a man sculling out on the river or an occasional long distance runner, perhaps; the charm of the blue and white spring day or yellow-brown-orange one in the autumn is not subject here to unseemly interruptions. You can muse in peace, and recall the river etchings by Haden and think of the three men in a boat, accompanied by Montmorency. There is a string of boathouses, a few of them delightfully Victorian; one is Gothic; most have balconies of wood or cast iron, and you can easily people them with nineteenth-century rowing men in caps and blazers and walrus moustaches. Ayling's, the boat builders, premises are especially pictorial. The 1953 high tide mark can be seen well up the wall; marks of this and earlier inundations are to be noted all along these reaches of the river.

The opposite shore is dull here, with little to see but the trees of the Bishops Park and the masts for floodlit football. Driftwood collects in quantity at Putney, and the ducks climb aboard it to preen their feathers. Empty cans, old electric bulbs come along in a strange waterborne procession, side by side with bottles, plastic drums, perhaps an upturned bed and sizeable baulks of timber. One could make a film of it by merely waiting and shooting as the strange conglomeration moves past. After the boathouses the embankment ends, opening out on to the broad, gravelled towpath, tree-fringed and countrified at Barn Elms, where Addison and Steele and other members of the Kit-Cat Club met in the eighteenth century in a house in the Park. Industrialized Hammersmith on the opposite shore appears as a fringe of wharves, cranes and barges, in complete contrast to the greenery at Barn Elms, where clumps of burdock, thistle and mallow grow luxuriantly by the river's edge (drawing on page 97).

Next, the Harrods Depository comes into view, terra cotta, pre-Great War; the wharf is overgrown with thistle and ragwort and the light railway line is almost obliterated. Hammersmith Bridge, recently repainted, is the subject of my drawing on the next page. Here again the feeling is that of an Impressionist painting, and I regretted at the time the drawing was made that I had no oil painting equipment to do it justice. The summer evening made colour essential; sky and water were suffused with an intense pale golden light, the river becoming a moving mosaic in blue and orange; the reflections of the bridge were disrupted by the breeze into a thousand different shapes of broken, brilliant colour, and the human element –

idlers, people gazing from the bridge, the rowing men launching their craft in the river – were all part of the mood of time and place, as the shadows lengthened and the trees across the river took on russet and olive hues.

The Lower Mall has a charming collection of Georgian and Regency houses with balconies overlooking the river, shadowed by limes, and lower down are elms planted by Catherine of Braganza, who was in the habit of spending some weeks here each summer for a number of years. After the Regency houses comes a pair of ancient cottages – worth a mint of money when they come into the market – in one of which lives one of the real old Thames watermen. Riverside pubs are the great attraction here – the Blue Anchor which has chairs and umbrellas on the Mall and a mid-Victorian bar fitting inside, and the Rutland, not much architecturally inside, but outside certainly one of the most pleasing Gothic pubs the Victorians ever built, all in pale greys, creams, pale greens and with black painted ironwork. The nineteenth-century Gothicists, in spite of their organization and the powerful forces they rallied to their cause, only partly succeeded in their attempt to make Gothic the prevailing style. Many architects remained unimpressed, but a few more designs like the Rutland, which is really only a modest affair, and the result might well have been instant complete conversion.

The Mall, once the fashionable part of Hammersmith and now all that remains of its former village seclusion, was divided into the Upper and Lower Malls by the Creek, crossed by a footbridge. Sailing barges discharged their cargoes at the Creek up to 1929. Gardens, made in recent years, now occupy the site, and are equipped with benches presented in memory of various people notable in the area, including General Booth. No doubt, he had his work cut out at Hammersmith, which was, in those days, very sharply divided into the gentry and quality and the proletariat. Working-class Hammersmith is an interesting subject for the London connoisseur, though outside the scope of this book; it can still be enjoyed to the full in the King Street area, the Broadway and the big town pubs and mean streets, though the new flyover has cut across the character of the district like a knife, as it has done at Chiswick. After much wandering, the thing to do is to take refreshment in Lyons, and look down on the crowds from the semi-circular windows, think of the productions at the Lyric Theatre and sample the dance hall. This is more satisfactory than meditating on the rapid carve-up of London to suit the traffic requirements.

Best of all, continue along the Mall to visit the Dove – the Doves, as it is more usually called – with low ceilings, dark woodwork, gorgeous blue and white beer pulls, Gillray type prints and an atmosphere Johnson, himself, would approve. Nothing is overdone, and the local flavour is still intact. In summer, the terrace is quite delightful; it is partly glazed over, and you can sit and enjoy your food and drink under the vine that spreads its tender green leaves below the glass, secure, like yourself, from the river winds that blow chill in the evening. Perhaps because of Kelmscott House and the Doves Press and bindery, I shall always get the

Hammersmith
Hammersmith

strongest Ricketts-Shannon Art and Craft reactions here, of no definite period and, indeed, mixed up with a Week-end Book-Albert Rutherston-Slade 1930 flavour not capable of exact analysis.

The Black Lion farther along, with its rose garden and skittle alley is, of course, pure *Water Gypsies* for there Sir A. P. Herbert, an immortal, is still to be seen in a corner of the bar. Over the coach-house of Kelmscott House is a quotation from one of the dullest and most absurd books I ever ploughed through, *News from Nowhere* by Morris, and above it is a plaque commemorating 'The first electric telegraph eight miles long constructed here in 1816 by Sir Francis Ronalds, F.R.S.' The coach-house was used for Morris's weaving at one period, and for Socialist meetings at a later time. You stand in front of the pleasant old Georgian house, looking almost exactly as it must have done when this remarkable man lived there between 1878 and 1896 – perhaps the variegated hollies, which grow so slowly, were there then – and wonder what he would think of the outcome of his visions? That the future Utopia he imagined, where men and women would be braver, happier, gentler, healthier and so on, would turn out to be merely the mixture as before?

However, it is very agreeable here in the summer; the river views, especially looking back to Hammersmith Bridge, present a series of Sisley or Monet subjects of people strolling under the trees, looking over the river walls, swans on the sunlit water, deep green trees, skiffs being carried from the boathouses, all under a pale sky flecked with the pink clouds of a summer evening.

Hammersmith Terrace is a curious barrack-like Georgian block, with little Victorian villas on the other side. Here the Upper Mall winds inland before return-ing to the river. A few modern houses have been pushed in among three storied Victorian terraces which have a pronounced seaside boarding house flavour. More Victorian terraces follow – overgrown, nineteenth-century Italianite – and then comes Chiswick Mall, a wonderful harmony of Restoration, Georgian and Regency architecture.

An afternoon in autumn is, I believe, the best time for Chiswick Mall, when sunlight is pale gold and a light mist diffuses it over the old, beautiful houses, allowing it to touch the geraniums, Virginia creeper, roses and hollyhocks with subtle colour. The scent of the autumn, pungent and sad like old woodlands in the memory, mingles with an almost indefinable smell – tar, oil perhaps, with a whiff of vegetation, but not unpleasant – coming off the water. Ducks are on the beach where the river runs cool and green by Chiswick Eyot, and they preen their feathers in the misty sunlight. The heads of the drakes flash a vivid bottle green. Ducks and swans enjoy a lazy river life, bottoms up in the water or leisurely inspecting their feathers, plucking an offending one out now and then, just so, while from the garden wall the robin twitters his plaintive Nunc Dimittis to the fading year.

These delightful houses, individual, yet grouped into a harmonious whole, are too good to be taken at speed. You need to savour their quality, enjoy the scenic

riverside walk and think at the same time of Walpole, Thackeray (Chiswick Mall is almost pure Thackeray yet, despite the jet planes above), and Barbara Villiens. At Chiswick one thinks of Hogarth (who, like Whistler, is buried in the church-yard), playing ninepins, accompanied by his pug dog, Pompey, and his pet bull-finch, Dick. The old village of Chiswick, centred on the church, has lost much of its peace since the opening of the motorway. There is a constant rumble of traffic and a continual procession of cars in the narrow street – doors banging, cars reversing, heavy lorries trundling through. Even so, blackbirds warble in the trees of the gardens, and goldfinches favour the churchyard where they pick off the seeds of snapdragon and ragwort.

There are two interesting houses here: the Burlington, almost opposite the church, and Ferry House – Tudor and Georgian domestic sharply contrasted. The Burlington, about 450 years old, was known for years as The Burlington Arms. The name was probably given to the place when the Earl of Burlington acquired

Chiswick House and much of the surrounding property from the Duke of Somerset. It ceased to be an inn in 1924. In recent renovations a coin from the reign of Queen Elizabeth I was found under a floor (illustration below).

Ferry House is a delightful late Georgian house of yellow brick, having the usual rectangular windows and white painted sashes and glazing bars, but relieved by a round headed window in the centre of the façade and a shallow curved arch on the ground floor. It is the subtle way in which the late Georgian domestic architects relieved uniformity without disrupting it which makes the style so attractive. They showed feeling, as well as a knowledge of the rules: this, and their command of proportions, makes all the difference between their work and that of later neo-Georgian copyists. The attractive façade of Ferry House is completed by a porch of two Roman Doric columns.

IX

The Pleasures of Kew

———— * ————

THOUGH the Burlington is no longer an inn, there are several riverside inns to be visited here: the group at Strand on the Green, for example, the Bull's Head at Barnes, if your tastes can comprehend a Victorian pub where jazz is the entertainment (it is actually a stimulating combination here) and somewhat farther down river the London Apprentice in Church Street, Isleworth. Isleworth still retains something of its old-fashioned rural appearance. Both the interior and exterior of the London Apprentice are of great interest. It takes its name from the apprentices of the City livery companies – often an unpredictable lot, it would seem, as light-hearted as present-day undergraduates: they used to row up river to Isleworth on their holidays. Isleworth had an importance as a port at one time. This character still hangs over the village.

I have described Strand on the Green at length in my book *London Overlooked*, but no amount of description can exhaust the pleasures of this narrow strip along the river. Its present exclusiveness with the correspondingly high cost of a house there (the contemporary style ones of Magnolia Wharf being the latest arrivals) is a comparatively recent development. Strand on the Green was an unregarded backwater at one time. The pleasures of the hamlet are entirely confined to the riverside and consist of comfortable pubs, delightful eighteenth-century and Regency houses, gardens and willow-lined towpath. Behind all this, in unbelievable contrast, are rows of grim terraced houses which properly belong to industrial Lancashire and dull blocks of flats of the usual London type of the 'thirties.

The views of the Thames on both the Kew and Syon sides are still unspoiled, if we except the outline of Brentford – a famous town at one time, the place of a battle in the Civil War and connected, too, with the crossing of the Romans under Caesar. Brentford to me is a no-man's-land, even though traces of its former qualities still remain to be discovered here and there among the shapes of the 1930s and 1950s, assuming its run-down atmosphere, approximating to that of Slough, does not deter the explorer from the start. For instance, there is a good nineteenth-century police station, not far from the gas works, in that grim Victorian style now being rapidly replaced. I prefer cop shops to be that way, just as I prefer coppers to duplicate those of the *Pirates of Penzance*: I hate them to be motorized, radio-controlled and efficient. There is a pawnbroker's shop of the eighteenth century, with delicate bow windows, some eighteenth-century terraced houses cut into below by shops, and better still, the very interesting pair of eighteenth-century Gothic oriel windows of wood, very decayed, that hang over a greengrocer's and an adjoining shop in the High Street. Both have ogee headed, sashed windows, but only one retains its Gothic traceried glazing bars. It is, of course, the Gothic of Walpole's Strawberry Hill – for amusement only.

Brentford Dock is worth visiting, if you like narrow boats, canal life and water gypsies who hang out their washing on lines stretching the length of the boat and who carry out various cleaning operations to the living quarters while in dock, usually watched by the kids and dogs who also favour a life afloat. There are a number of interesting views worth seeing: the trim tubs and flower beds associated with English canal architecture, narrow boats, the backs of old houses and the ancient church tower among the trees.

And for the conveniologist, there is the gents' lavatory at Kew Bridge. The interior is quite splendid; this alone making a visit rewarding. It is equipped with two six-sided glass tanks (B. Finch and Co., Lambeth) and curly ornament. Each tank is supported on brass columns rising from the stalls, the ensemble being one of the most interesting and well-preserved lavatories in the west of London and safe, I hope, from modernization and interference.

Now that London has become so unromantic and barrel organs a rarity in its streets, it may well be that City slickers are no longer impelled to visit Kew in lilac time, and, as for the Dorian nightingale, he has probably pulled out long ago, like his relative in Berkeley Square. Still, I think there are two other reasons why one ought to visit Kew about the middle of the month of May, which is the peak of bluebell time around the Queen's Cottage in the Royal Gardens, and in the depths of winter, say on an ice bound day in January, when there is extra pleasure in visiting the tropical houses and savouring the contrast between the green and scented warmth within and the bleak and forbidding prospect of the world outside.

The gardens are full of delights, even for those not horticulturally inclined: magnolias in the spring, sweeps of daffodils that would surely reconcile Wordsworth to urban life, interesting items such as a thorn bush of the same species as that from which the Crown of Thorns was made and sometimes, if you are lucky, you will encounter vague and irritating old women jerking about behind some huge opuntia – these ancient females complete the bizarre quality of the experience and compensate for the Pagoda, which is intriguing from a distance but dull and disappointing when seen in close-up.

Kew is unquestionably eighteenth century in feeling, and yet it is chiefly attractive to me for its late Victorian houses. To own one of these was once an ambition of mine – crowded out, I am afraid, by too many other ambitions – but the idea remains fresh: that gothicky house of yellow-grey brick, the garden with the monkey puzzle, funkias and fernery, the conservatory with the tiled floor and stove plants.

The very name 'Kew' suggests such things. I would pass through the hall door of stained glass with birds, corn and rushes on it in brown and yellow, and mount up to the snuggery to gloat over my Burne Jones and Rossetti drawings, to read the poems of William Morris and Swinburne, to pretend I believed in progress, in the inherent decency of things, and to read old copies of *Punch*. I should also read Richard Jefferies in the sequestered walks of the Botanic Gardens, and come home to shrimps and watercress. For absolute perfection, the house would be filled with Venetian blinds and gaslit, haunted, too, as an added refinement by the ghost of a half-starved Victorian governess.

On the opposite bank, facing Kew Gardens, is Syon House, surmounted by the famous lion removed from Northumberland House when this palace of the Strand was demolished in 1874. It is an eighteenth-century view of bosky foliage, great cedars and flowering meadows. The towpath walk to Richmond is pleasantly rural, especially when the chestnuts which overhang the river are in flower. The Thames has now shed the last suggestions of being a working river and, by the time one arrives at the half-tide lock, the pleasure boating atmosphere of *Three Men in a Boat* predominates. Above the railway bridge, the towpath is a riverside promenade, where the water weeds cluster thick at the river's edge. Dogs and their owners bake themselves in the afternoon sun, and here you may dream a lazy afternoon away, while the wash of the passing steamers plashes among the dock and cow parsley – that is, if you take care to keep well away from the transistorized maniacs, who make the afternoon hideous.

On a hot day, a blue mist hangs over the town, the grass is cut as close as a billiard table and the heat is too intense for all but the sparrows who cheep at the river's brim. Although the promenade lawns are of ample size and few idlers were about at the time, while I was making this drawing, a dreadful middle-aged

couple found it necessary to sit down next to me and tune in to a commercial station, intent, as it seemed, on making life unbearable, until I told them to go to hell. I could forgive her (I told them) her diamanté rimmed spectacles and double chins, for these were simply English Gothic; I could forgive him, just about, his close cropped hair and loud, open-necked shirt; I could, with an effort, overlook his sandals; but the wireless was an infernal machine, an insult to the bright day and charming riverside and I declared my intention of chucking it in the river to cool it off.

These transistorized fiends are fast becoming a distressing nuisance on all the reaches of the river where one could formerly anticipate peace and easy hours on a sunny day. Such drawbacks apart, Richmond is ideal for the Londoner, and undoubtedly the most satisfying way of getting there (if time is too short to make the journey by river) is by the seventeen mile line from Broad Street to Richmond, which has been saved from closure. The Broad Street platform is large, flagged and cool, with an atmosphere like that of a cathedral. The leisurely Victorian mood is very strong; there are rare mirror advertisements for Peterson pipes and Abdullah cigarettes. Besides, there is a working model of a passenger locomotive, late 1880s, of the North London Railway, though you don't get much movement for a penny. With luck, you may well find yourself in an ancient stuffy carriage, the better to enjoy that scenic journey. Through Hackney, you go, Dalston and Canonbury – the last with a popular art garden with a cannon among the trellis and flower beds. Many of the stations on the line, twenty in all, are in a pleasing state of decay. They are rich with unused waiting rooms, superannuated gas lamps and broken windows. There is talk of brightening them up: I hope this is an unfounded rumour. The aim should be to deepen that air of desolation, which is the true glory of English travel. . . .

The whole journey is the finest railway experience in London, with the panorama of St Pancras at Caledonian Road seen among the gasometers and factories and the wooden Gothic station at Kentish Town as highlights. You look down at the churches sticking up above the flats and endless terraces, and actually see horses and carts in the streets. There is ragwort growing in the sidings at Gospel Oak. As if this richness were not enough, there is S. S. Teulon's church of St Stephen, at Hampstead, and a succession of backyards, washing, eccentric sheds and rhubarb at Acton and Willesden. Finally comes Kew, followed by Gunnersbury and then Richmond, with the sun shining on a river, calm as a pond, under a sky of pale cobalt blue.

X

The View from Richmond Hill

——— * ———

RICHMOND (a favourite place with the Tudors), in spite of the influx of coffee bars, jazz record shops and brassière depots, still retains much of the mellow qualities imparted to it in the eighteenth century. Conscious efforts have been made to retain this, notably in the National Provincial Bank, damaged in the war and recently rebuilt. The Bank had a wine shop as part of its ground floor. Over the shop spread a choice old vine, planted over a century ago. Great care was taken to preserve it during the rebuilding – the new bank, as it were, being *brought up* to the vine, which once more flourishes on the corner and puts out its grapes.

Georgian doors of good quality are scattered all over the town, even in the main shopping street, and there are delightful alleys of mixed Georgian and Victorian architecture leading to Richmond Green. The Green has some of the finest eighteenth-century domestic architecture in Surrey, and there are few more satisfactory ways of spending an afternoon than under the shade of its trees, watching the dogs and the people they own ambling over the grass. There is one utterly delightful house hung with wisteria – a dentist's house, if I remember rightly: mysterious dispensation of Providence that equips dentists, doctors and lawyers so unfailingly with the best the Georgians could achieve!

There are good Victorian town pubs in Richmond, too, besides those on the river, and old cottages of humble origin, but now advanced in status, in unexpected corners.

Richmond is notable to me for possessing an eighteenth-century picture palace. This is the Gaumont in Hill Street. The cast-iron canopied entrance belongs to its earlier career as the Royalty. I am particularly susceptible to buildings that were originally something else – warehouses and bingo halls that began life as chapels, or vice versa, cafes that were once pubs, churches transmogrified into houses and so on. London is full of them, and this Richmond cinema, I think, heads all the rest. While on the subject of places of amusement, I must not omit the Richmond Theatre at a corner of the Green, a captivating late-Victorian design in terra cotta, small in scale, but handled in a fine theatrical style. It is precisely what the exterior of a theatre ought to be, and was designed by Frank Matcham.

103

Opposite the cinema is the Pâtisserie Française, all the more valuable in times like these when elegance is out and all that is raucous and nasty distressingly in. Its tea services are of period character, and have the name of the firm in a Victorian cartouche, in black and white. Inside the shop are glass counters lined with trays of chocolates, nougat and sugared almonds. A delicate scent of fine chocolate meets one at the door. In the window are more chocolates, violet creams and bonbons all displayed on glass shelves supported by iron brackets of art nouveau design. Needless to say, there are mirrors and those glass sweetmeat jars of the golden age. One hardly ever sees them in use nowadays: they have gone to earth like the cachous they used to contain. Dogs are not officially admitted to this establishment, though I pleaded hard for mine and he so charmed the proprietor that she melted like one of her own confections, presenting him with a chocolate and an invitation to have tea there again next time he was in Richmond.

Fully appreciative as I am of the gimmick in its multitudinous forms, of the no-event or contrived occasion, I view the tendency to insinuate these public relations fantasies into restaurants with less enthusiasm. Eccentric settings might, on occasion, be a means of distracting one's attention from the food one is buying. In one riverside eating place in central London I found my appetite entirely discouraged by the bosoms of the Nell Gwynn waitresses; such distraction is, I feel, demonstrably unfair. In any case, restaurant gimmicks have been much overdone, apart from their built-in appalling quality, and for those who simply want superb food, well served in plain, honest surroundings, I recommend Valchera's, near the Richmond station. It is one of the few remaining Italian restaurants of the old school, with little to distinguish it on the outside from an ordinary café. The Café Royal and Romano's were originally of this genre; the grandeur came later. The bar at Valchera's is at the back, the traditional position for a bar in this kind of restaurant – a tradition to which even the celebrated Rules in Maiden Lane subscribed in the 1890s. The walls of Valchera's are lined with mirrors; there are honeysuckle hat and coat stands and art nouveau cruets that throw up a trumpet shaped centre to contain flowers. It is well worth coming specially out to Richmond to dine here – that is, if besides period atmosphere, you want genuine old-fashioned, interested service, and food and wine to match. Max Beerbohm once made the remark that, whereas in the West End you dine more reasonably than you had expected, in Soho you find it dearer than you thought; but at Valchera's, after a course of West End eating, your wonder is that the place has not been discovered by the food writers and written up long ago; you wonder how it can be that you are dining so well and so comfortably so close to London.

One of my favourite Richmond perambulations is along the riverside to the meadows at Ham, with river, trees, grass and charming architectural vistas all the way. You can start by St Helena Terrace, early nineteenth century, of yellow brick and white stone, with a range of boathouses under its balcony by the river, and perhaps take in refreshment at the White Cross Hotel which has a Doric portico and umbrellas and tables on the terrace; also, if the time of year is right, a delightful, lithographed poster displayed on the side wall – a lady driving tandem (advertising, of course, the Richmond Horse Show). Where the river bends at Water Lane is a roughish looking eighteenth-century warehouse with a tiled roof, forming an interesting contrast to what the Victorians would call the neatness of the surrounding terraces and gardens – a fragment of industrial revolution archeology with an eighteenth-century, creeper-covered house next to it.

Richmond Bridge is one of the finest on the Thames; it was designed by James Paine, opened in 1777 and widened between the wars, its architectural character being carefully preserved. The stretch from the bridge, alongside the terraces and eighteenth-century houses now turned into hotels, is one of the most varied and interesting character. There are one or two snack bars with metal tables and chairs under the trees, filled on hot evenings with replicas of the figures Rowlandson drew. Fat old women wash down pork pies with vividly coloured liquids; they are accompanied by their heavy husbands and rounded females with sturdy infants. By the landing stage and the boathouse, sun-tanned characters sit in chairs under the verandah, their cloth caps shading their eyes. These men seem to be emancipated from the necessity of earning a living; at all events, they sit easy, some of them in wooden arm-chairs, surveying the river, profoundly critical of the prowess of those on it. Other men in jerseys attend to the needs of those who come to hire boats.

The jury under the verandah have now a new case to consider, for the ferry boat is slowly pulling out with a middle-aged couple on board. He wears a panama, she a blue and white spotted dress and outsize glasses; they, too, are English Gothic and the jury know it. Six or seven pairs of eyes follow them as the boat pulls out, with easy strokes, into midstream, noting the wonderful complacency of the waterborne pair; as the boat touches the Marble Hill shore, Charon, with a gallant air, helps the lady out and holds the elbow of her unsteady consort, who holds down his panama with one hand, lest the breeze off the river commits it to the deep. Another half a dozen strokes or so, and the ferryman is back again to the sloping weed covered embankment below the jurymen. They, however, have lost interest in his case, having delivered their verdict to their full satisfaction: another object claims their attention in the shape of a steamer on her way to Hampton Court.

Farther along, at the University of London Club, a crew of hairy-legged stalwarts prepare to take to the water, and a number of tycoons in natty boating rigs are messing about their superb craft – as shipshape as if just delivered from the Boat Show – and their decorative women take up slinky poses, conscious of being appreciated by the lesser mortals on the towpath.

The Three Pigeons (drawing over the page) is another of those exactly right Victorian riverside inns of mixed Gothic-Swiss extraction, very agreeable to see, especially when its tea garden is full of family groups, all enjoying themselves on a

WATNEY

THREE P[

RICHMOND ROYAL
HORSE SHOW
1928

The Three Pigeons Richmond
J S Fletcher

golden evening when the river meadows beyond are rich green and lush, the cattle graze contentedly as the shadows lengthen and a pale moon hangs over Richmond long before the sun has set.

A walk up Richmond Hill is best made at this time. The terrace gardens slope down to the Petersham Road, and from here is one of the most famous views of the river. Windsor Castle, about fourteen miles away, can be seen when the day is clear; the rich woods of the Thames valley lie between. The Terrace gardens once formed part of the grounds of Buccleuch House, and were purchased for the public in 1886. Turner, de Wint and many other artists have painted the view. Across the river, Turner found two of the river subjects from the Liber Studiorum: the Claude-like 'Twickenham, Pope's Villa', based on one of the artist's finest monochrome drawings (a subject in which a pair of splendid trees, elms presumably, are reflected, along with a circular garden temple, in the calm river) and the 'Young Anglers', an incident evidently seen by the artist, himself a dedicated fisherman, near his home, Sandycombe Lodge.

Richmond Bridge, itself, was a Turner subject: young ladies and gallants picnic on the grass, the bonnets and parasols cunningly repeating the arches of the bridge. In the distance, a sailing barge is moored at the old warehouse by Water Lane and the wooded heights rise in the distance above the bridge. Those heights are now capped by the Star and Garter Home for men disabled in the Great War, built on the site of the Star and Garter Inn, famous in the Victorian period. This I never see without reflecting on the disgusting shift to the observance of Armistice Day on the nearest Sunday to 11 November instead of on its original occasion, right historically as well as emotionally. This sacrifice of principle to expediency makes one ashamed to be English. The building also reminds me of an old man I once knew who not only sinned against the light by playing the cello but also wore the same Flanders poppy each year, despite the increasing dustiness and dilapidation of his investment. He would wear the poppy and play the cello at the same time. His goldfish would leap clean out of its bowl and have to be reinstated – not at the iniquity of the poppy; it was the slow music in a minor key that touched his fishy heart.

I have done a good deal of sailing at one time and another on the Thames, but one day, when I was working on this book, the heat was intense by the river. The sun shone fiercely from a sky that looked like bright blue glass. The pug dogs and Cairn terriers on the grass are quite unable to move; other breeds managed to loll out their tongues. Bald-headed men mopped shining domes with handkerchieves. I thought of Rossetti's poem 'Downstream'; I thought the river would be cool and kind; I thought of the three men in a boat and, of course, Montmorency; I thought I would give up work, take a speedboat and make my way to Eel Pie Island to eat and drink in the shade of the willows and enjoy the view of Twickenham and its charming old houses by the ferry. I asked the man if the boat were in good shape and had not been handled by incompetents recently. He told me they were all incompetents who hire boats – every one of them. Thus assured, I kicked off.

It was one of those days so rare in England. Even on the river there was hardly a breath of wind; the ducks floating on its surface were fast asleep. My imagination began to get active before long, and I pictured myself first as Sir Henry Seagrave and then as a lonely adventurer on the Amazon, seeking a lost civilization. Next I saw myself as the pilot of a Mississippi steamboat heading for Natchez, with a cargo of Southern belles and Mississippi gamblers, racing the Robert E. Lee, getting every pound of steam from the overtaxed boilers. At this point, the engine coughed and gave out. Nothing I could do had the slightest effect. The fuel tank was full. I supposed the thing had got somehow overheated. Anyway, there was I, helpless in the boiling sun, not another boat in sight. Then a wasp appeared. What the hell he was doing there, I never knew, but I could not rid myself of him, any more than I could start up the engine, and I drifted crazily into the path of a steamer. I managed to avoid being run down or overwhelmed by the backwash – how I shall never know. The oar made no progress against the cross current of the turning tide, and it seemed I was destined to stay there all night. Eventually, a speedboat came along, and its owners gave me a tow back to my base. By this time I was crazy with thirst and streaked with sweat and oil. As my helpers sped away under the rising moon, I heard one say, 'Those silly buggers ought not to be allowed on the water.' His friends replied, 'No, a clot like him would have even bloody well sunk the Ark.'

The boat's owner was apologetic. He said it did occur on occasions – the conking out. A thought struck me as I walked away to clean off the oil and grease, so I turned back and said, 'By the way, you ought to rename that boat of yours.'

He said, 'Oh, what to?'

I replied '*The African Queen.*'

The reach of the Thames to Kingston, about four and a half miles, flows between the residential districts of Richmond, Twickenham, Strawberry Hill and Teddington, all much sought after in the eighteenth century and full of associations with the period, especially social and literary. In those days, the river was of secondary importance. To Twickenham especially came the aristocracy, writers, wits and dilettanti: Pope, Gay, Reynolds, Johnson, Kitty Clive, Garrick – everybody, that is, who counted in eighteenth-century London. Horace Walpole's toy Gothic at Strawberry Hill was far more than a dilettante's bauble; it played an important part in confirming the tentative interest of the eighteenth century in Gothic forms, romantic concepts, so assisting, at no matter how great a distance, the creation of an outlook in which a Gothic Revival became possible – I nearly wrote inevitable. Strawberry Hill is a convent nowadays, and remains an important study for all those interested in the history and strivings of nineteenth-century Gothic.

Eel Pie Island, the subject of a bucolic drawing by Rowlandson, is about eight acres in extent. It seems to get less and less attractive, few of its buildings being of a high order. But Twickenham is worth visiting, if only for its eighteenth-century church where Pope is buried:

> Heroes and kings your distance keep,
> In peace let one poor poet sleep,
> Who never flattered folks like you,
> Let Horace blush and Virgil too.

The well-known Pope's Villa is, of course, the Victorian successor to the poet's own house which was demolished early in the nineteenth century.

Teddington is the point where the Thames ceases to be tidal, and here the jurisdiction of the Port of London Authority ends and the Thames Conservancy Board takes over. The old lock, still in use, is dated 1857. A summer evening is the time to see it, for then the lock is bright with flowering plants, the water is sparkling and brilliant in blue and gold, and the lock is busy. Then, especially when the steamers crammed with passengers in summer rig are locking through, the evening breeze gently flaps the awnings on the top decks and the swans glide under the sunlit trees, you recall the more halcyon passages of Jerome's book or perhaps think of those long summer evenings when the story of Alice was told in the water meadows at Godstow – when it was always next time. Though boaters, blazers and parasols are a rarity, Teddington Lock on a summer evening is still a subject for an Impressionist painter: Sisley, Monet or Manet ought to have painted it in the great period.

Summer evening Teddington Lock

The village of Teddington, long and straggling, is not particularly interesting, apart from the old church of St Mary, with a squat, brick tower of the eighteenth century, where Peg Woffington is buried, and its mossy ivy-grown churchyard. There are one or two attractive old shops, including a charming old pharmacy, in the village street. Opposite the old church and in strong contrast to it is the huge Gothic Revival church of St Alban the Martyr, unfinished, a smaller version of Lancing Chapel dropped down in Twickenham.

The river is somewhat dull between Teddington and Kingston, unless, being incurably romantic, your sensibility runs to wooden bungalows. The chimney stacks of the power station add little to the prospect, though its buildings are well screened by gardens, flowering trees and shrubs. The Victorian Gothic boathouse of the Kingston Rowing Club is worth seeing, opposite the little islet where boats are moored. The club-house is of yellow and red brick, with generous trimmings of cast iron and carved barge boards in that agreeable chalet style which first appears at Putney and several examples of which remain on the upper reaches of the Thames, a few being highly ornate.

As you approach Kingston on the towpath, the Surrey bank is lined with the floating homes of neo-Chelsea Bohemians; the boats, a miscellaneous collection also in the Chelsea manner, are drawn up at low tide by their sterns on the shingle. Washing flutters in the breeze, and plants – geraniums and nasturtiums – grow in unlikely containers such as coal scuttles.

On the Hampton Wick side the towpath ends at Kingston Bridge. Wharves and lumber yards take its place and a number of Victorian, Georgian and a few modern houses, with lawns sloping to the river and gardens planted with ilex, willows and prunus.

Kingston Bridge (opposite) was built in 1828 and widened, though without spoiling its appearance, in 1914. The far bank on the Hampton Wick side is lined with chestnut trees. The broad walk by the water's edge is charming on a summer evening, when the river is a pale bright blue and flecked with blue and white sails. Old-fashioned motor boats, with fat ladies under the awnings, chug up the river, and the proprietors of smaller launches invite the courting couples, family groups and transistor-carrying youths to take to the water. 'Any more for Hampton Court – boat just leaving.' Even the cranes and industrial buildings across the river seem co-ordinated into the harmony of the scene, their outlines softened by the golden light. Ducks quack, oars, plied by uncertain hands, squeak their protests, and the lemonade and sandwich man does a roaring trade.

Kingston is one of those not quite spoiled towns of Surrey, but the impress of the wrong kind of London life is strongly on it. Only round the Parish Church and Buttermarket can one visualize its pleasant country town aspect as it was before the suburban Londoner closed in with his big stores, multiple tailors and beefburgers. Boots, the chemists, and the Griffin Inn are two of the ancient buildings worth seeing, as is the old Town Hall with its quaint statue of Queen

QUEEN BEE

Kingston Bridge

Anne in the market place. The narrow streets of the Buttermarket retain a medieval character; the wonder is that they have not been cleared away long since. There is also the Parish Church with its great square tower. These apart, the chief attraction of Kingston is the riverside which confers gaiety and interest to an otherwise increasingly dull and suburban town.

It is not a great river, as rivers go, but it brought London into existence. By comparison with the scenic rivers of other countries, the Thames might be considered homely, unexciting, yet Turner, Whistler and the Impressionists painted it. The *Golden Hind* was once moored on it, the *Mayflower* was built on its riverside and the little ships once went down it to Dunkirk. Caesar and Shakespeare gazed on it, and Wren brought the city raised on its banks to a perfection undreamed of in a single lifetime.

It is a river of ever changing moods, greatly varying character and magic distances – the unentailed property of all who love London. A Royal river it may be, but it belongs as much to the seedy youth who loiters over London Bridge, where the movement of ships and running tide stirs the Anglo-Saxon imprisoned in the town-made boy.

The part the Thames has played in the greatness of London and that of the English race is beyond calculation. It is the oldest and newest part of London.

O Love, what need have you and I
Of vine and palm and southern sky?
And who would sail for Greece or Rome
When such a highway leads him home?